Sustainable Tourism:

A Destination

Managers Perspective

Dr. Cheryl Venan Dias Ph.D.

ISBN: 9798357346599

DEDICATION

This book is dedicated to my little one Joanna.

CONTENTS

ACKNOWLEDGMENTS

I would like to thank my husband **Venan Bonaventure Dias**, who shaped my career into what it is today, hand holding so that I don't deviate from my goal, I am blessed by his presence in my life.

How to use this book

Fact Files

Fact files is a collection of information about international organisations that are the ultimate authority to define the tourism terminologies. A text that is accompanied by this image will include important details about its year of inception, headquarters, and their major function and contribution to the body of knowledge.

Key Learning Point

A key learning point summarizes the essence of the unit in discussion. It serves as a point of reference to recall the contents even after reading the entire book.

For Learners

The method of using this book is to first read the objectives of the chapter before attending the classroom session and also watch the videos suggested at the end of the chapter. This will give the learner an idea about what is the expected learning outcome from the given chapter. During the course of the class or reading the learners will be given key learning points that can be further used for discussion and debate in a classroom setting. All students should make an active effort to complete the case study or a class activity either as an individual assignment or in a group.

For Facilitators

Suggested pedagogies will make the classroom session more interactive, the key is to make learners prepared for a class that is engaged, it is not just the prep time by the facilitator but also prep time from the students. All this will be included in the facilitators check point. The facilitator can refer to the learning objectives and ensure that towards the end of the chapter the learning is measured through an evaluation in form of quizzes, case analysis, written test or presentations.

For Managers

The suggestions given for the learner can also be used by 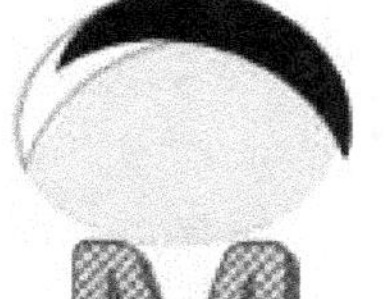 the manager, however it is suggested that the managers look for the managerial implications section which will give you a direction in solving managerial problems associated with tourism. Associated case studies will enrich the ability of the managers to manage such problems in real life situations. Managers have to think on their feet, encourage their team members, support them during testing times and also when deadlines are to be met. It also includes a section where decision making skills will be honed as well as provide a worksheet to delegate the task among their members.

1 PARADIGMS OF SUSTAINABLE TOURISM

About the Chapter:

This chapter introduces the reader to the concept of sustainable tourism and its importance. Moreover, the term sustainable tourism is used so frequently while promoting tourism products, while in reality, it is quite distant from the core concept associated with the triple bottom line. If we look at the concept in the light of sustainable development goals, the idea gets more clarity.

Chapter entails:

- Sustainability is it just a cliché?
- The inception of tourism and travel
- The Indian subcontinents perspective about tourism and sustainability
- Tourism and sustainable development goals (SDG 2030)
  - Key learning points
  - Facilitators checkpoint
  - Managerial implications

Tracing the Origins

The first instance where a tool for travel was identified was in Mesopotamia with the invention of the potter's wheel somewhere around 6000 to 4000 B.C. The wheel has come a long way from hand drawn carts to the most modern levitating trains with no wheels. Man was always smitten by wanderlust, the documented evidences are from sailors who travelled the world for trade and commerce. A Viking explorer Leif Erickkson discovered Greenland and New Foundland in the 11th Century. In a quest to discover East India, Christopher Columbus persuaded the Spanish Royalty to fund the first voyage in 1493, he eventually discovered the Caribbean or the West Indies (History, 2020). A Portuguese nobleman Vasco-da-Gama successfully navigated the Cape of Good Hope in Africa in 1498 he arrived into Calicut present day Kozikode on the west coast of India. The major mode of transportation was the sail boats, the trade and commerce between the Middle East and India was dominated by the traditional Dhow's the major commodity for export was the spices and indigo powder which was used prominently as a dye.

After the successful flight on the first heavier than air aircraft in 1903 by Wright brothers at Kitty Hawke North Carolina, US, travel from east to west coast was possible. The early days of air travel were highly regulated by the government. While in the 1990's airline deregulation allowed private players to enter the system and this made travel cheaper due to the introduction of low cost carrier (LCC) such as the South West Airlines founded by Herb Kelleher in the US. While in India, Air Deccan founded by Captain G.R. Gopinath became the leader of LCC across the Republic of India. While travel by air and cruise became popular for trade, colonisation and for educational purposes. The invention of the steam engine in Europe gave rise to the steam powered locomotive engines and promoted the railway network. The British introduced the railway systems in Africa and in India and currently in India the railways have become the lifeline of travel systems for the daily commuters.

As the travel industry had its steady share of growth. Inns and monasteries allowed travellers to sojourn for a while before they carried on with their journey on foot or on the beast of burden. Traverns in Europe were popular joints that merchants would frequent for a drink and to rest from their tedious journey. The concept of hotel and restaurants emerged later as a commercial option based on the need for a traveler to rest, and as a home away from home. Now accommodation sector is a trillion dollar industry worldwide with popular brands of hotel chains across the world. While food and beverage also became an essential service along with the accommodation. Development of various cuisines to attract the traveller also became prominent. The accommodation sector, customer service associated with it, the food and beverage sector are collectively called the hospitality industry.

The early travellers were a privileged few especially the ones who were able to visit the Mediterranean to escape the cold winters. Grand tour was introduced however not everyone was privy to this luxury (Chaney, 2000). A tour was considered to be a luxury good and was enjoyed by few who could afford it. The first official travel agent of the British Royal Armed Forces was Richard Cox, who then founded the Cox and Kings travel agency in 1758, they were also the general agents to the regiment of Foot Guards in India (Cox and Kings, 2020). While in 1841 Thomas Cook and Son started the first leisure company for the British and started his first commercial packaged tour in 1845, they were the first to have a printed guide of the itinerary and cost effective means of railway tickets. Thomas Cook is believed to be the inventor of modern tourism (Britannica, 2020). The closest to a foreign tour enjoyed by common man was during the First and the Second World War where they were sent to foreign soil and they got to see new places that were ravaged by war. With the development of modes of travel came the opportunity for many to be part of these modes as employees in housekeeping, flight attendants, reservation and ticketing, tour operators and tour managers. They became the source of employment for many and improved the economic standards of the employees.

In the later part of the 20th century the influence of information technology on tourism was observed, the traditional tour operators and travel agencies had an online presence and were now called as online travel agencies (OTA). Software as a service (SAAS) was exploited the most by the travel and tourism industry. They promoted their business through business models such as business to business (B to B) and business to customer (B to C). Expedia became the world leader of B to C travel service providers by 2014, they had acquired hotels.com, hotwire, trivago, Expedia, Cruise Ship Centers, their revenue was well over USD 14 billion (Expedia Inc. 2013). Apart from the online travel agencies, the Global Distribution Systems (GDS) are software that provide services to travel agencies that can help them book air, car, train and hotel rooms for their passengers. Currently there are four service providers who are quite popular among travel agents Travel Port which owns both Galileo and Worldspan which is quite popular in India, While Sabre provides services to the airline industry as well as to travel agents in the USA, Australia as well as UAE. Amadeus which is quite popular in Europe.

As travel and tourism evolved the means and modes of transportation were able to shorten the distances travelled. Along with the advent of the faster modes of transport issues such as pollution, carbon footprint, depletion of resources such as fossil fuels, and increase in cost also were the consequences. Currently the industry is looking at fuel efficient modes of transport and wants to cut down on fuel that can negatively impact the environment.

Divide the class into four groups and provide a flip chart to each group. The learners should be able to use the mobile or laptop as a learning aid during this activity. Assign some prominent continents to the group such as North America, Africa, Europe and Asia ask the students to create a time line of the earliest mode of transport in that area to the modern means of travel developed in that area. The group should present the findings before the classroom.

Create the google classroom online and share the classroom code with the learners, solicit participation from learners, ask them to turn-in the work suggested for learners regularly. The session can be graded or just as a class activity. Load the suggested videos on Google classroom for learners to review before classroom discussion.

The Indian sub-continents perception about tourism and sustainability

The earliest reference to tourism in India can be found in the texts written in Sanskrit script. Three terminologies are closest to the modern-day terms used in tourism. The term used for travel was Atna. Where Desh Atna meant travel outside the country for trade and commerce, Paryatna which meant travel for purpose of leisure, and TeerthAtna which was associated with Pilgrimage or Religious purposes. Travel was mostly by the beast of burdens ideally the bullock cart, or horses, camels, and elephants. British who colonised India introduced the motor vehicle, the railway line which connected Bombay now Mumbai to Thane. In Goa, the people belonging to the higher income group would travel in a Palquin which was carried by servants. Buses were also introduced by the Portuguese and this offered a source of income for the entrepreneurs operating the services. Travel by sea route was also taken up by the people in the colonial era where they traveled to the other Lusofonic cities such as Zanzibar, Kenya, and Nairobi before moving to the United Kingdom.

The first flight was operated by TATAs who flew in the mail between India and Pakistan. Due to the intervention of the Prime Minister of independent India (Late) Pundit Jawaharlal Nehru this airline became a publicly owned organization and was known as the flagship carrier of India, Air India. Air India operated the international routes for India while Indian Airlines operated the domestic sectors. Many players came up such as East-West Airlines, which was started by Thakiyudeen Wahid which suffered losses and was eventually closed for operations. However, deregulation in the industry in 1990 allowed new players such as Jet Airways and others to enter the Indian Air Space. After the Liberalization, Globalization, and Privatization (LPG) in 1990 by the then Finance Minister Manmohan Singh, FDI was permitted in India giving scope for Indians to take up jobs within India than traveling abroad for work. Bangalore became a hub of most of the travel process outsourcing companies and even the GDS's all the four GDS are currently serviced by Indian nationals from Bangalore, Karnataka, and Mumbai, Maharashtra. The GDS are also used in travel process outsourcing (TPO) and call centers which are associated with airlines such as American Airlines and Emirates Airlines.

India faced two recessions once in 2008 and lately in 2019 which saw a decline in the productivity of some airlines such as Jet Airways which faced financial losses, Air Deccan was taken over by King Fisher Airlines and later stopped operations. Indigo Airlines, Spice Jet and Go Air are currently dominating the Indian skies with Air India planning on going private. Vistara a TATA venture has emerged lately and is performing impeccably. On the railways' network front investments are now made to develop dual tracks, the single-track system created a lot of delays for the existing railway system. Faster trains are now introduced such as the Tejas. There are luxury trains that operate some circuits and are quite popular among foreign tourists namely the 'Palace on Wheels' and 'The Deccan Odyssey'. Monorail and metro rail are introduced in the major metros of India and are the favorite mode of transport for the working class in India.

In 2016 the Public-Private Partnership model had developed a new cruise berth in Mormagao Port Trust, Vasco-Da-Gama Goa, there has been an increased number of shore excursions in Goa. With the latest edition to the luxury cruise liner and developed in Italy, the Karnika is the first Indian Cruise liner which caters to the Indian crowd launched in September 2019 after its bankruptcy post pandemic it started a fresh as Cordelia cruises. The routes are domestic and international with the international itinerary covering Mumbai-Muscat-Dubai-Bahrain and back. The Cordelia cruises now operate the shorter routes between Goa and Mumbai, and longer routes from Chennai, Colombo, Maldives, Goa and Mumbai. The accommodation sector also has seen steady growth from the 5th to the 12th Five Year plan. International hotel chains and brands that are existing across India and also provide career opportunities for many Indian graduates. The authentic hotel accommodations are existing in form of Palaces, Hawellis, and Bungalows which are partly converted into a hotel for the upkeep of the property.

After 2012 the National Planning Commission was dissolved and was replaced by National Institution for Transforming India (NITI) Aayog a government 'Think Tank', though it does not have the power to impose policies and it has given up the one-size-fits-all schemes adopted by the planning commission (Parekh 2018). The major aim of the government through its implementation is to become the enabler. NITI Aayog is mandated to monitor, coordinate, and ensure implementation of the Sustainable Development Goals. NITI Aayog undertook the extensive exercise of measuring India and its States' progress towards the SDGs for 2030, culminating in the development of the first SDG India Index (NITI Aayog, 2019). India is taking steps towards change and also aligning itself towards the 17 sustainable development goals set up by the United Nations. Among the 17 identified the ones that were earmarked by UNWTO through their internal assessment were SDG 8, 12, 17. The SDG Index with regards to these goals will relate to tourism (Dias, 2020).

NITI Ayog, (2019) at the national level SDG 8, the goal of decent work and economic growth, India emphasizes on stable macro-economic growth, improvement of business, and skill ecosystem. The Index scores of all states of Republic of India and union territories are at an average of 65. Also a special mention is made about sustainable tourism development to create jobs and promote culture as one of its goals which have to be achieved by 2030. At a National Level SDG 12 Sustainable Consumption and Production, India accounts for 17.5 percent of the world population, while it occupies only 2.4 percent of the world area, this mandates a policy framework which is efficient in the achievement of resource efficiency, reduction in waste and pollutant activities, and focus on renewable energy resources and technology. The travel and tourism industry banks heavily on fuel and when cleaner energy is used it can reduce the carbon footprint on the entire planet. SDG 17, Partnerships for the Goals though identified at an International level is excluded at a National Level due to unavailability of comparative data across the states, this is one of the areas which is identified as a gap, which can prove detrimental to all the ambitious plans as partnerships, communication at a global level also can affect the way sustainable tourism takes shape in India.

Travel and tourism have grown exponentially in India, and the five-year plans contributed towards the growth and establishment of the accommodation sector in India. There is a need to manage fuel efficiency and switch towards economically feasible and environmentally healthy fuel such as renewable sources namely solar-powered or hydrogen-powered equipment. The number of vehicles that ply Indian roads is particularly diesel-powered and contributes heavily to the carbon footprint and also harms the environment due to the Particulate Matter 2.5 or PM2.5 emissions which can cause health hazards to humans, flora, and fauna. This beats the entire idea of SDG 2030 so strong policy changes are mandated to impact the environment positively.

Sustainability is it just a cliché?

The advent of COVID 19 reduced all forms of travel around the world. Earlier strains of viruses were isolated cases that were specific to certain regions such as the SARS, Swine Flu, Bird Flu, and even the dreaded Ebola. While the current strain is so vociferous that its outbreak reached to every corner of the world and has put a halt on tourism activities. Domestic and international travel and tourism services have come to a standstill. This is the time to reflect on what can go wrong when nature is tampered with. As a destination manager a pertinent question arises i.e. Will the tourism businesses survive the onslaught of this virus? Many of the small and medium enterprises may perish or may reinvent, innovate, and thrive.

But the very nature of tourism is to bounce into its tracks after a setback due to political, environmental, or economic crisis. Political exigencies spell out wars and policies which may curb or restrict travel to certain areas.

Environmental issues that can prevent travel can be due to natural disasters such as the one that the world is currently engulfed in, floods, earthquakes, tsunamis, and other climate change-related issues. The economic crisis is due to the political decisions and environmental effects which can result in an economic slowdown and even cause a recession. The current pandemic also has created a deferred demand for travel due to the lockdown of entire cities across the world. This is one such time where destination managers have the time to reflect and set the strategies for their business when things turn back to normalcy.

The biggest contributor to carbon footprint is the travel industry, though tourism is deemed to be a smokeless industry as service delivery takes the center stage. While the travel industry especially air travel is the largest contributor, it was grappling with the problem of grounded aircraft that used lithium powered engines which posed technical issues for the aircraft, now the solution has arrived, the move is now towards hydrogen-powered aircraft as this is considered to be the future fuel for the industry and has zero emissions. There are two schools of thought about sustainable tourism. Some scholars believe that sustainable tourism is a unique construct and stands apart from contemporary tourism, while the other group believes that all forms of tourism should be sustainable. To understand the term better it is better to look at the concept through its definition and its boundaries.

Some international organisations of travel and tourism have provided us with some profound definitions of sustainable tourism development. Some prominent names are IUCN and the UNWTO.

 IUCN also known as World Conservation Union1, it was conceptualized in the year 1948 with a conservationist from around the world with headquarter in Switzerland. They grew to 855 members in 134 countries by their 50th anniversary in 1998. Currently, they have 208 state and government agencies as their members, 1100 plus NGOs and indigenous people in their network, over 15,000 experts in natural resources, more than 160 regional members across the world. It is a global organization with expertise from a network of science and conservation specialist. The association includes governments, international agencies, state authorities, non-governmental organizations, volunteers, scientists, environmental lawyers, resource administrators, and grass-root ecosystem managers. They are an international advocate for ecologically sustainable development.

---

[1] IUCN(1996) https://portals.iucn.org/library/dir/publications-list accessed on 30/03/2020

IUCN was the first to define sustainable tourism development with an overture towards the promotion of conservation as:

> 'Environmentally responsible travel and visitation to natural areas, to enjoy and appreciate nature (and any accompanying cultural features, both past, and present) in a way that promotes conservation, has a low visitor impact, and provides for beneficially active socio-economic involvement of local peoples.' (World Conservation Union,1996)

UNWTO a legal entity of the United Nations was formed in 1975. It promotes responsible, sustainable, and universally accessible tourism. Its foundations are based on the triple bottom line which is to be the driver of economic growth, inclusive development, and environmental sustainability. It aims to support the tourism sector by advancement in knowledge and promote sustainable tourism policies worldwide. Its secretariat is headquartered in Madrid, Spain. It has 156 member states, 6 associate members, 2 permanent observers, and 400 plus affiliate members. Their priorities are to improve tourism competitiveness, promote sustainable tourism development, poverty reduction, knowledge sharing, and capacity building, and building partnerships.

UNWTO has defined sustainable tourism development with a focus on the present and future needs of indigenous stakeholders and visitor satisfaction as:

> 'Sustainable tourism development meets the needs of present tourists and host regions while protecting and enhancing opportunities for the future. It is envisaged as leading to the management of all resources in such a way that economic, social, and aesthetic needs can be fulfilled while maintaining cultural integrity, essential ecological processes, biological diversity, and life support systems.'

If we examine both the definitions we can observe a three-pronged approach first being the concept of tourism as a socio-economic activity which is encouraged both in the present and future, using due diligence in promoting responsible travel and visitation to natural areas. The second is about the conservation of natural heritage and the maintenance of biodiversity2. The third being the socio-economic needs of the host regions to be met. This is not possible without proper management of natural resources. However these objectives should not be a one-time activity, it has to be a perpetual one that requires human resources to maintain the processes associated with tourism. Which reaches out to the social, economic, and environmental requirements of the host region that promotes tourism. We can call the

---

[2] World Tourism Organization. WTO Website "Sustainable Development of Tourism: Concepts and Definitions". Retrieved 30/3/2020, http://www.world-tourism.org/frameset/frame_sustainable.html.

system self-sustaining when continuous monitoring of the activities and the impacts are done. While risks related to tourism activities are mitigated and corrective action is taken regularly. The need to travel is not just for the present, tourists' prefer to revisit a destination in the future too. Their experiences for the future visit also should be factored in while monitoring the footfalls at the tourism destination3.

 Ironically the world treats sustainable tourism as a unique construct, while in reality, all forms of tourism should follow the tenets of sustainable tourism. The basic three premises on which all forms of tourism should be developed are the people; which include both tourists and residents, the profit; the economic benefits to be derived by the residents, the planet; the natural heritage, and biodiversity of the destination. Which has to be conserved, preserved, and protected for future generations.

Other contributors to Sustainable Tourism Development

Apart from the IUCN and UNWTO, three additional international organisations are authority on sustainable tourism development. They

---

³ Linking Communities, Tourism & Conservation, A Tourism Assessment Process
Eileen Gutierrez, Kristin Lamoureux, Seleni Matus, Kaddu Sebunya (2005)

conduct market analysis and provide support and liaise with the industry, the government think-tanks, and lobby for the benefit of the tourism fraternity.

As a destination manager it's advisable to constantly update your knowledge about the tourism dynamics by researching educational content from their website with regards to impacts on your destination. Destination managers can also become members of international bodies to increase the credibility of their destination. Destination managers are also advised to apply for accreditation programs and memberships to chapters to receive regular communication about the travel and tourism industry and to raise the standards of the destination.

WTTC, World Travel, and Tourism Council were founded in 1990 in collaboration with American Express. It is headquartered in London. It is represented by chief executives of multinational accommodation, cruise liners, catering, MICE, transportation, and other travel-related services. It's predominantly a private-sector lobbying group that conducts in-depth studies on global tourism impacts. One of the significant contributions of WTTC is the 'Blueprint of new tourism' that encourages the government to adopt sustainable tourism policies. Another contribution was the 'Open letter' to the Heads of States and Government to accept the importance of travel and tourism and its challenges. UNWTO and WTTC have collaborated to form the 'Global leaders for tourism campaign'. Its role is to create awareness of jobs across the sector and its impact on GDP. Their priorities are security and travel facilitation, crisis preparedness and response, and sustainable growth4.

Pacific Asia Travel Association (PATA) 5was founded in 1951, and based in Bangkok, Thailand. Its membership includes 100 government, state, and city tourism bodies, 76 airlines and cruise lines, around 2000 companies and organizations, 17,000 Individuals, and 36 active chapters worldwide. It acts as a catalyst for the responsible development of travel and tourism for the Asia Pacific region. It also enhances the sustainable growth, value, and quality of travel and tourism in partnership with private and public sector members. It provides unrivaled data and insights related to inbound and outbound statistics, it provides an in-depth report on strategic tourism markets. It assists its members in securing revenue due to new businesses every year. PATA also

---

[4] WTTC, https://www.wttc.org/priorities/ (2020)
[5] PATA, https://www.pata.org/about-pata/ (2020)

contributes to the sustainable and responsible development of travel and tourism in the Asia Pacific through the protection of the environment, conservation of heritage, and support for education.

Global Sustainable Tourism Council (GSTC) was founded in the US as a not-for-profit organization, to promote sustainable tourism around the world. It provides international accreditation for sustainable tourism certification bodies. They have two sets of criteria one being the 'Destination criteria' for public-policy makers and destination managers, while the 'Industry criteria' is for hotels and tour operators. They also help to set up the minimum criteria for a tourism business or a destination, which will enable them to protect and sustain the world's natural and cultural resources. It ensures that tourism meets its potential for conservation and poverty alleviation.

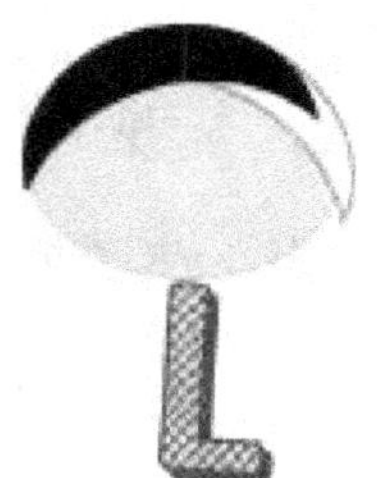

Identify the role of WTTC, PATA, and GSTC in defining sustainable tourism use the footnotes to trace the websites to these organizations. Trace the definition back to IUCN and UNWTO and discuss additional contributions from the three international organizations. Identify a tourist destination in your locality and discuss among your group if the triple bottom line stands to benefit from tourism activities in that area.

 Assess the area as per the IUCN and GSTC criteria and identify if this certification can be applied in your area. Initiate the certification process by getting the buy-in from the National Level and Regional Level tourism bodies. Identify the other means to raise funds for this certification. Apply to crowd fund platforms to raise funds.

Paradigms of Travel and Tourism

If the definitions of sustainable tourism are transferred into a model, we would arrive at the basic premise of sustainable tourism as the triple bottom line or the triple p's. Which is associated with people, profit, and the planet. While in definition they stand alone, it should be noted that they are well complemented by other paradigms which are related to the geographer's point of view, tourist types, behavior and motivation, host behavior towards tourists, marketing perspective, and experience generation. It is suggested that the destination managers link the base model with the existing models of tourism to study the effects of tourism in totality.

Sustainability Paradigm

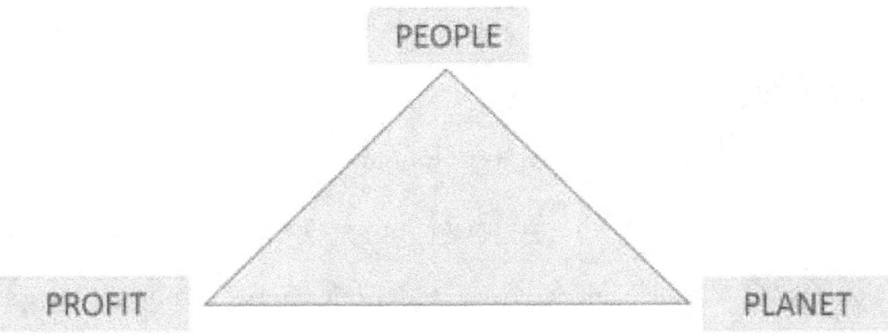

Source: Author, 2022

If observed minutely, the dimension of people has two associated sub-dimensions to it which can be termed as the host or the resident population at the tourist destination and the other the tourist who visit this place. The planet dimension can be looked at in terms of the geographer's perspective and the environmental perspective. The profit can be measured in terms of the economic gains and benefits that the tourist destination may have based on tourism-related activities. Some of the economic benefits are auto-generated when a tourist arrives at the destination and some may have to be induced by the efforts of a destination manager or by policy changes by the national and regional bodies that overlook tourism activities at the destination. The sub-dimensions can be now linked with the associated paradigms which if managed efficiently can have positive impacts on the destination.

Sub-Dimensions of Sustainable Tourism Paradigm

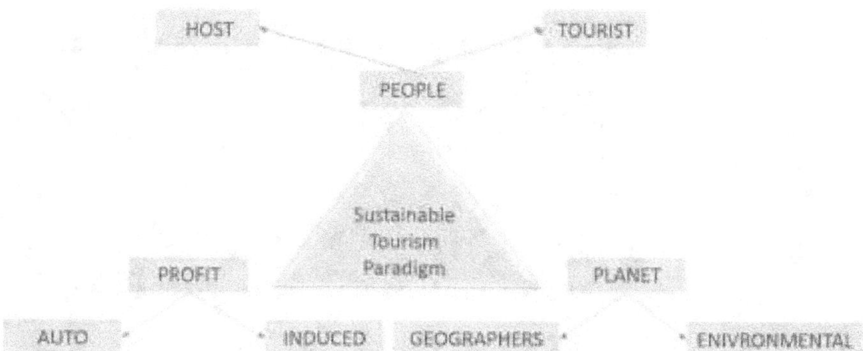

Source: Author, 2022

PEOPLE

The Host

The host or the resident population is governed by multiple paradigms associated with tourism. The list is exhaustible, however for brevity only four dimensions are selected which will be most appropriate for the learner of tourism and for the destination manager to tap the local resources optimally. The top four models which will be discussed in this section are Traditional Knowledge, Local Destination Network, Social Innovation, Doxey's Irridex.

Paradigms associated with the host population

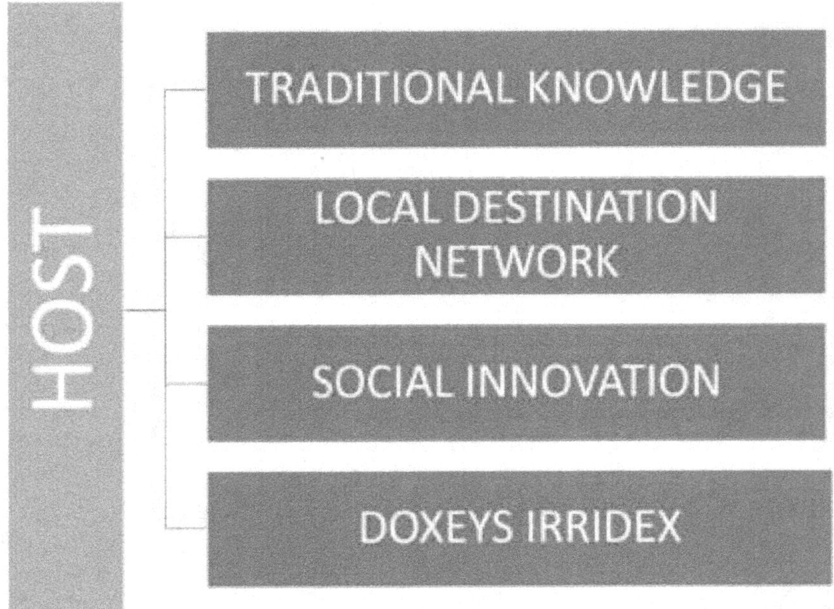

Source: Author, 2022

Traditional Knowledge:

The task of a destination manager begins with proper research of the area where the destination is being developed, without providing authentic experiences high-end tourist may not be attracted to such areas. Some of the well-kept secrets of the land belong to the people of the land. Which can be translated to traditional knowledge. It encompasses knowledge, innovation, and practices of indigenous or local communities living around the world. It is a build-up of experience gained from centuries of knowledge, it is well adapted to the local culture and environment. This knowledge is handed down through the ages orally than in form of a script it transcends down the generations of these indigenous people. The ownership is collective and can manifest itself in form of stories, songs, folklore, proverbs, cultural values, beliefs, rituals, community laws, the local language, and agricultural practices, including the development of plant and animal breeds (UN Convention on Biological Diversity)

A definition provided by the International Institute for Sustainable Development states that,

> 'Traditional knowledge is information, skills, practices, and products-often associated with indigenous peoples- which is acquired, acquired, practiced, enriched, and passed on through generations. It is typically deep-rooted in a specific political, cultural, religious, environmental context, and is kept as a key part of the community's interaction with the natural environment.' (IISD, 2003)

While the World Intellectual Property Organization does not attribute this knowledge to be ancient they believe that it can be evolving regularly. They do believe that it has several subsets such as 'indigenous knowledge', 'folklore', 'traditional medicine' and others. The traditional knowledge can be a periodic process and might become a daily process when the community members have to face some challenges presented in their social or physical environment. It can be contemporary knowledge that is embedded in traditional knowledge systems. Which each community can develop and maintain in its local context.

Case study:

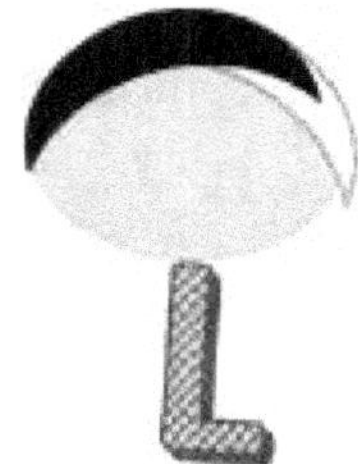

Grampurush is a spiritual entity that is part of the traditional folklore of Goan Villages in India. Each grampurush has his own identity and a name. The folklore of gramprursh is carried on in Goa so that new methods or ignorance do not surpass the traditional knowledge of the village forefathers. It is believed that storm water drains are the pathways of the gramprush and should not be blocked by construction or by landfilling, it is attached to a reward and punishment, the punishment or misfortune befalls anyone who tries to block the storm water path. It is true in one way as blocking the path can cause unwanted flooding in residential areas. Goa is known for the 20,000 km of built heritage called the 'bunds' or ancient embankments, the grampurush is said to protect the village of the bund breaches. To date, the sluice gatekeepers are warned if there is any breach in the bunds, which can result in the flooding of the village. There are certain villages in coastal Goa especially the Candolim, and Calangute belt where the people still believe that the house will not sustain if they are built more than the first floor which holds even today. The local villagers still follow this unwritten rule without fail.

1. What is the subset of traditional knowledge that is depicted in this case study? Are there any elements of sustainability that are discussed here?

2. Why was it necessary for the forefathers of Goan Villages to tell this story to their generations to come?

Local Destination Network (LDN)

The tourism network is considered to be an important tool for economic development at a destination. Sustainable tourism stands to significantly gain from a proper tourism network development by promoting inclusivity of community and commercial interest (Gibson et. al. 2005). It is also advisable to adopt appropriate network performance indicators to ensure a healthy network lifecycle. The local destination network is made up of actors such as the community members, educationist, start-ups, entrepreneurs, funding agencies, financial institutions, local governance, and regional level governance. Tensions may arise while trying to get these actors together due to differences of opinion about the community and commercial value sharing propositions.

> 'The Scottish-Scandinavian Discussion Group has defined a network as, a set of relationships between individuals acting in an organizational and/or private capacity to achieve a particular purpose; such networks may be of three types: formal, semi-formal, and informal.'

Types of networks

Type of Network	Membership	Aims and objectives	Interaction
Formal	Formal actors Examples: Regional Tourism Organizations	Predetermined and identified	Social, Valued, Subordinate to formal aims.
Semi-formal	Formal actors Example: Local business marketing consortium	Predetermined and identified	Equal importance as formal aims.
Informal	Informal members Example: Neighbour hood host families network	Absence of clear goals	Social purpose and exchange of information

Source: Adapted from Lynch 2000, tabulated by Author

A tourist destination can get popular due to social media interventions, movies, and travel blogs. The major issue is when mass tourism occurs without proper network development the economic benefit to the communities may not occur. Commercialization may only bring more social ills and irritate the local communities. The need for any community residing at a potential destination is job creation. If this benefit is withdrawn from a business model there is a possibility of friction and an ill-developed destination which may be on the verge of collapse and decline. Any network needs a catalyst and a binding cement that will ensure that there are no gaps while developing a destination. Local network development should have learning and exchange, business activity, and community as its basic benefit criterion areas. It should be developed on natural and built systems that exist at the destination. Without focusing on these areas tourism is bound to fail.

Benefits of Local Destination Networks – Tripartite approach

Learning and Exchange	Business Activity	Community
• Transfer of Knowledge • Tourism education process • Communication • Cultural values • Acceleration of implementation of support agency initiatives • Facilitate the development of small-scale enterprises • Facilitation of innovation • Staging and development of tourism experiences • Usage of community level pedagogies for knowledge sharing • Knowledge of financial support	• Co-operative activities and value chains • Enhanced cross-referrals • Talent development • Increased visitors • Use of SME's and support agencies • Visitor season extensions • Increased entrepreneurial activities • Inter-trading within networks • Enhanced product quality and visitor experience • Business development opportunities • Repeat business	• Fostering common purpose and goals • Community support for destination development • Increases the sense of community • Engagement of SME's in destination development • Increased job creation • Increased opportunities for community level entrepreneurships • Inclusiveness in sustainable tourism policy building • Promotion of traditional knowledge • More income staying locally

Source: Adapted adapted from Lynch et al. (2000) based on a review of Adam (1994), Buhalis (1994), Buhalis and Main (1996), Evans (1999), Hankinson (1989), Houghton and Tremblay (1995), Huang and Stewart (1996), Litteljohn et al. (1996), Lowe (1998), Lynch (2000) and Morrison (1994, 1996), Dias, C (2016, 2017, 2019). Tabulated by Author

Now that you are aware of the types of networks and the tripartite benefits of local destination networks, use the given tableand collate and analyze data associated with the success indicators for LDN.

LDN Success Indicators

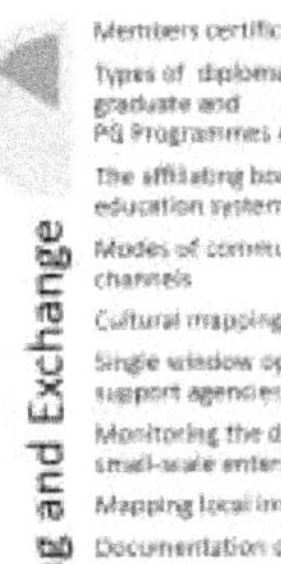

Source: Adapted from Gibson 2005 for business activity, tabulated by Author

Provide local, and regional sources of data from the local library or college library database, also source data from tourist information centers, tourism corporations, and associations which can enable the learners to analyze the data further and develop as a research paper.

Social Innovation

Though the term innovation is widely used in all industries, it had a mixed reaction from administrators and philosophers of that day, during the 5th century BC from its Greek Origins it was also known as Kainotomia, innovation meant to cutting into afresh or making new (Godin 2012), it also meant change something that was written by law and it meant that people would break the law to do something new or maybe dilute the process of the original methods. In the early 20th century innovation is mostly attributed to the works of Schumpeter who was also known as the 'Father of Innovation Theory', it was associated with factory products and technological improvements. Later as the service industry such as hospitality and tourism developed it was imbibed into services as well. Though services are not tangible, they can be experienced emotionally. Freire et. al. (2019) suggested that social innovation in contrast with technological innovation promoted sustainable practices that reduced or stabilized man's environmental footprint, and social equity and economic development.

Social Innovation is the value created by the interaction of tourists and the local communities. (Sørensen, 2007) defined social innovation as a collaborative process that benefits from networks, co-operation, and co-production. Some of the immediate benefits are changes to social interaction and practices, followed by the social development of communities (Mosedale and Voll, 2016). Ideally, it is a technique that helps to solve societal problems. Some of the basic societal problems are the distribution and sharing of wealth, the disparity between the rich and downtrodden, and the distribution of food. While in the context of tourism it would be problems associated with ownership of a destination and its heritage, communication between networks, creation and distribution of wealth due to tourism, and sharing of wealth and resources.

Case Study

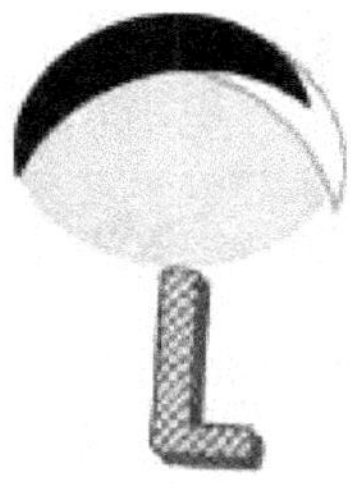

It is interesting to know that even in the early 5th Century BC Xenophon a Greek philosopher provided innovative solutions related to the labor shortage post-war in Athens, he suggested financial incentives to private slave owners and also encouraged starting an organization, in which private individuals would combine resources in business which would enable them to share the wealth and minimize risk. (Amemiya 2004, Xenophone 2020, Dupont, 2017).

1. What were the potential post-war societal problems that Greece would face?

2. Do you feel that the suggestions provided by Xenophon were innovative enough to solve such problems?

3. What the plans that you would suggest to increase wealth, share the wealth, and minimize risk at a tourism destination in the light of the above case?

Doxeys Irridex

The change in the attitude of the resident population towards tourist and tourism development in different stages of the destination's life cycle is termed as Irritation Index or Irridex, this was established by Doxey in the year 1975. The theory assumes the negative socio-cultural impact of tourism on the local population residing at a destination. There are four stages of Doxey's Irridex namely; euphoria, apathy, irritation, and antagonism clearly explain the deteriorating responses of the residents to the tourist arrivals at that destination. The first stage of euphoria is when the footfalls at the destination are small and the local community welcomes tourism. During the stage of apathy, the relationship between the host and the tourist gets formalized through tourism policies. The significant growth of arrivals and competition for resources becomes a growing concern among the host population and leads to irritation. At the stage of antagonism, the residents blame all the social ills on the uncontrolled growth of tourism.

Paradigms associated with Tourist Arriving at a Destination

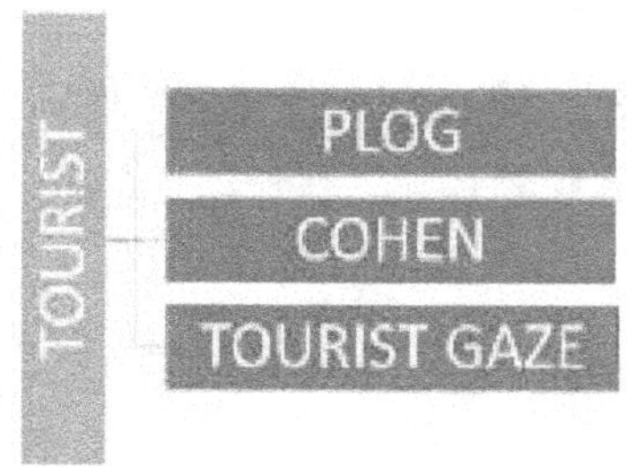

Source: Author, 2022

The Tourist

Plog's Psychographics

Destinations may not remain the tourist favorite perpetually, their demand rises and falls, these fluctuations are attributed to tourist and their psychographics which does not change along with the destination visited. Psychographics are associated with the tourists' attitudes, motivation, lifestyle, personality, and intra-personal issues. Plog divided the tourist into a continuum or a normal curve. The model designed by Plog can be used even for the development of tourism destination, it can be also compared to Butler's Tourism Area Life Cycle (TALC), to understand the life stage of the destination and the type of tourist who is attracted to it.

The motive behind Plog's research was the backing of sixteen travel-industry clients, that included foreign and domestic airlines, aircraft manufacturers, and renowned publishers who wanted to know the reason for people not to travel by air. By 2001 Plog published an invited paper with Cornell University. Which revealed the personality type of tourist and their choices. Plog divided the tourist into two Archetypes namely Allocentric and Psychocentric, Where 'Allo', means 'varied from', while 'centric' was the 'focus', by its terminology we can affirm that allocentric or venturers, they are a tourist who prefers off-beat destinations which are virgin, have few visitors, they prefer to purchase local products, and also dwell with residents. While the psychocentrics or dependable have a high rate of anxiety while traveling away from their home, they prefer well-developed destinations, crowded areas, with established hotels, and eateries, they travel with a lot of luggage to feel at home, they prefer to travel by their vehicles. While the travelers in between are followers of one of the archetypes.

Plog's Psychographic Personality Types

Source: Plog's (2001) Model of Venturers Vs Dependable

Cohen's Typology of Tourist:

Another classification of tourist was given by Cohen, he divided the tourist into:

- The organized mass tourist

- The individual mass tourist

- The Explorer

- The Drifter

The organized mass tourist prefers the environmental bubble, they prefer a pre-packaged tour, try to avoid contact with local people. They believe that institutionalized travel is more preferable over self-curated travel experience. In the case of an individual mass tourist, who shy away from crowded experience both from other tourists as well as local people, this type of tourist also prefers the environmental bubble but has a preferred choice of destination. The explorers abandon the environmental bubble, and organized the trip on their own, they also prefer a comfortable and clean place to stay even on a shoe-string budget, they get uncomfortable when things get tough. The drifter completely abandons the environmental bubble, there is no planned itinerary, they live with the local people, they may work and pay for their necessities, they live close to local people and immerse themselves in the culture.

Tourist Gaze

In a quest to have an authentic experience, the tourist places a set of expectations on local populations while participating in heritage tourism. A tourist arrives with some set of expectations about the destination and sets the gaze on monuments, landscapes, local lifestyles, and cultural attractions. The cultural authenticity that the destination held with its heritage and history is completely overridden when the locals try to conform to the expectations of the tourist. The once authentic experiences delivered to tourists are replaced by staged experiences that the locals conjure. This happens when the tourist who may be a 'dependable' typology expects something from back home at the tourist destination. Be it local music that they would listen to at home, and the tourist would expect the locals to mimic and reproduce the same. Urry (2002) asserted that a tourist spot can lose its authenticity over some time or its sacredness. It is also a stage which is familiar to the residents, but becomes unfamiliar to the visitors and thus turns attractive, activities which are mundane become extraordinary in the local settings.

PLANET

The geographer's point of view

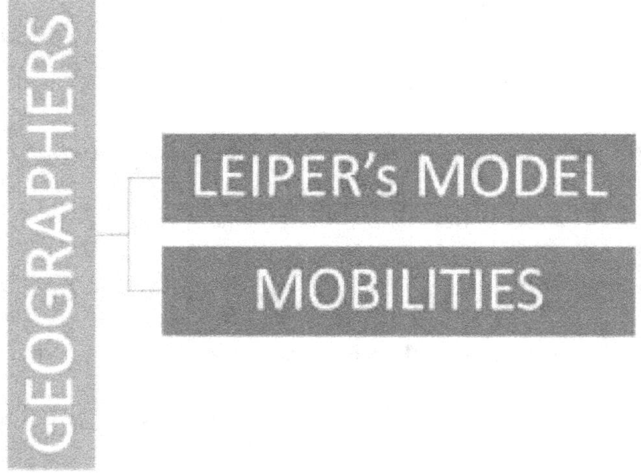

Source: Author, 2022

Leiper's Model

Geographers viewed tourism as per the spatial use of a destination for tourism purposes, including the movement of tourists from one location to another. Leiper in 1979 proposed a model which was modified in 1990 that involved three areas which the tourist traversed namely the tourism generating region (TGR), the transit area (TA), and the tourism destination region (TDR). What divided the person from a TGR and TDR is the distance, cost, and also availability of other options. When a transfer of a person happens between the two major regions the transit area may also tend to benefit from the movement. Another model that supplements Leiper's model is the gravity model, the attraction to the tourism destination region is very strong and can overcome the constraints of cost, distance, and inconvenience.

Mobilities Paradigm

Researchers have identified two facets of the mobilities paradigm one being the Sedantarist and Nomadic, mobilities are not limited only to the use of the mode of transport for movement but also the communication that gets mobile due to the use of telephone, internet, and wi-fi. While the Sedantarist may be limited to travel the geographic boundary and maintain the purity of travel to their geographic area. While the nomadic traveler may go beyond the political boundaries. Sheller and Urry 2006, differentiated between places and visitors, specifying that places can have a push or pull factor, while they are immobile, the visitors to it are not. The traveler can be involved in activities such as talk, work, or information gathering, it may involve being connected or having a moving presence with others. At present, there are machines that aid mobility such as GPS and Geo Tracking devices that aid in human mobility.

The environmental paradigms

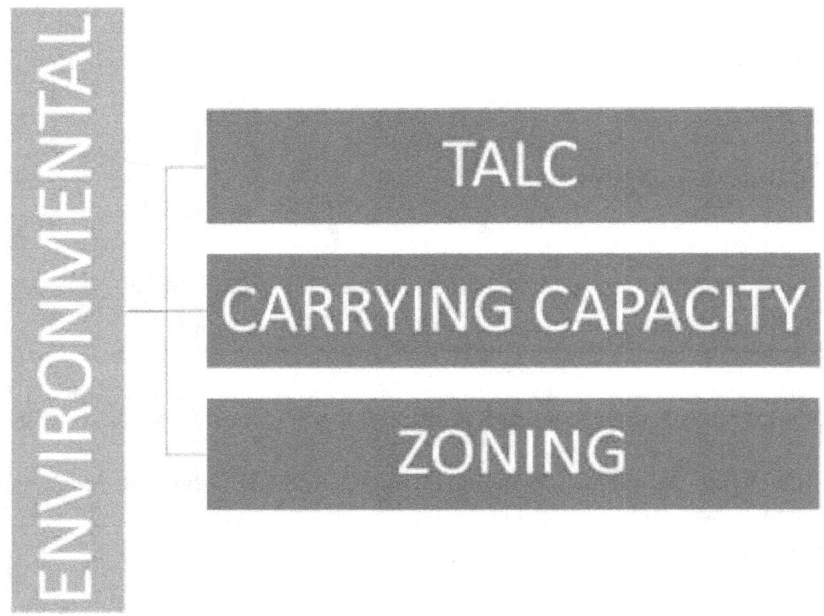

Source: Author, 2022

Tourism Area Life Cycle (TALC)

Tourism area life cycle is the six phases that a destination passes through while evolving as a tourism destination, this was first proposed by Butler in 1980 and is being widely used by research scholars to study the life stages of destinations. The six phases of evolution are exploration, involvement, development, consolidation, stagnation, decline, or rejuvenation. At the exploration stage, no tourists visit such places and they would not even have the required amenities and infrastructure to support tourism the type of tourist who would prefer to visit here would be the Allo-Centric or Venturers. As the destination gets more familiar it enters into the next four stages, while for destination managers it is these stages that need to be treated with care and involved in planning to arrest the faster evolution of the destination. When the Dependables enter this zone we can imagine that the development has reached its pinnacle and it no longer appeals to the Venturers. There is a competition for resources and the destination enters into its decline stage. If it can de-market and revive itself it may enter into the rejuvenation phase.

Carrying Capacity

Studies on carrying capacity were extensively studied since the 1960s. As tourism grew the concern of its impact started emerging among academia and policymakers. This construct was an attempt to define the limits of tourism growth and development at a destination. Carrying capacity may be defined as 'the maximum number of people that may visit a tourist destination at the same time, without destroying the physical, economic, socio-cultural environment and an unacceptable decrease in the quality of visitors' satisfaction' (UNWTO 1981: 4). Further explanation of the acceptable limits was discussed by Getz (1983) wherein carrying capacity was split into six categories: physical, economic, perceptual, social, ecological, and political. Kennell (2016) explains how the six categories of carrying capacity boil down to what is the maximum extent to which a tourist can use the resources at the destination before physical settings get degraded. Over-dependence on tourism for economic gains can topple the economic carrying capacity. Perception of the destination as it turns into an overcrowded location affecting the perceptual carrying capacity. The excessive intrusion of tourist which creates negative feelings of the resident population towards tourism and disrupts the social carrying capacity. Degradation and permanent damage to the environment through its effect on flora, fauna, and geographic alterations thus affecting the environmental carrying capacity. Political instability due to land-rights and tourism income control which can negatively impact the political carrying capacity.

Zoning

To prevent disputes due to cultural, demographic, ethnic and religious beliefs, designated areas were ear-marked to enable men and women to enjoy their leisure time without interruption. This was a trend observed from mid-19th century. There are two types of zoning which are based on social segregation and type of activity. Examples of social segregation are observed in Egypt which promoted females only beaches which enabled them to bathe without being observed. Italy promotes women-only beaches which excludes male-oriented activities in this area. Abudhabi has family beaches and women-only beaches which provides for exclusive beach areas for such groups. Iran has beaches with fiberglass barriers and water sprays for women beachgoers.

Activity based zoning:

Hazardous Activities	Socially Conflicting Activities	Other Conflicting Activities
Horse Riding	Smoking	Dog walking and fouling
Sea and shore angling	Beach parties	Diving
Sand Yachting	Loud Music	Swimming
Boat Launching/sailing	Alcohol consumption	Fires and barbecues
Motorised activities	Naturism	Camping
Surfing	Beach sports	Climbing
Kite Surfing/buggies	Motorised water acti.	Running
All-terrain vehicles	Group activities	Kite Flying
Frisbee and ball games		

Source: Author, 2022

Activity zoning allows for leisure tourists who has conflicting areas of interest from the regular beach users, their areas are only reserved for such activities as depicted in the table depicted above.

Paradigms of profit

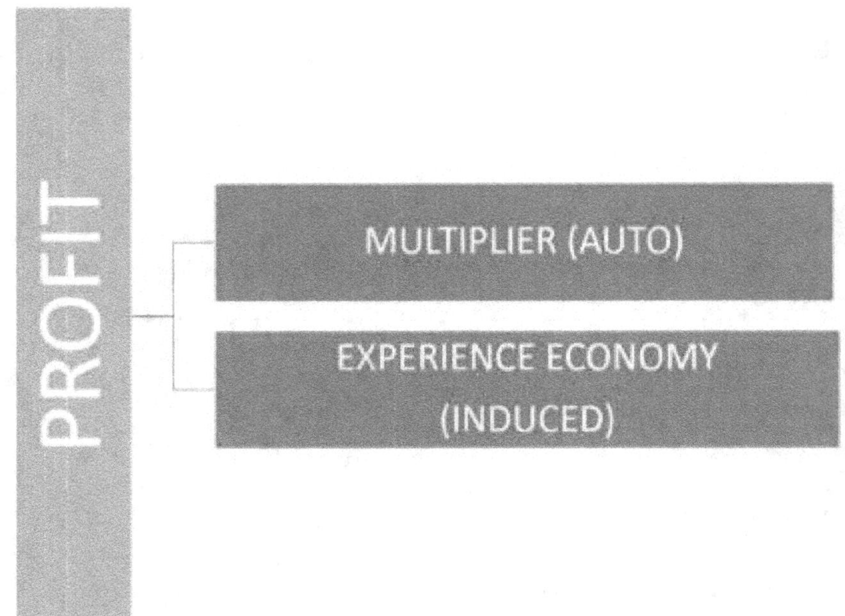

Source: Author, 2022

Multiplier Effect

The tourism multiplier effect 6is the proportion in which the money spent by tourists in one country becomes a source of income to people living in a region. The money thus infused through tourism changes hands multiple times till its value becomes so minuscule that it becomes impossible to follow it further. Inflation on the one hand can harm the multiplier effect as the

---

[6] Modified extract from Opinion section written by author on 26th November 2013 on Herald News paper.

money that comes in through tourism can be used only for limited purposes, in contrast to a time when the currency is strong and can purchase goods and provide added value to the consumer. In turn, it also provides the other suppliers with a source of income and enables them to spend and contribute towards the country's economy.

The following are the main leakages that affect the multiplier effect in tourism:

--The expenditure on import for tourism purposes, including building materials and décor.

--Import of supplies to run various facilities offered to the tourist.

--Import for consumption by foreign tourists such as branded beverages.

--Remittance of profits on foreign capital invested in the tourism industry.

--Cost in foreign currency of conducting market activities abroad.

The lower the value of the multiplier, the lower is the benefit to the domestic economy from tourism. Some suggestions that could help in reducing leakages through tourism based policies are:

• Reduction in journey routes by having proper communication and dialogue between service providers and the respective authorities.

• Promoting and marketing local brands and providing incentives to handicraft shops and malls that implement this.

• Recognition of people who make austerity their lifestyle in delivering quality services through their businesses.

• Encouraging investment in infrastructure-related systematic plans and protecting the funds of investors by providing them options.

• Recognition and encouragement of youth and individuals researching clean sources of fuel, and provision of government backing and grants for such research.

To conclude, the tourism multiplier is a direct reflection of the leakages that occur through imports and also through savings that are not invested in banks and other financial institutions. Small and incremental changes in our behavior made in this way can contribute significantly to improving the economic standards of the destination.

Experience Economy

Understanding the theoretical framework of experience production within the experience economics gives insight about a tourist who has experienced or received an experience during a tour. Thus allowing destination manager clarity on how to create or offer the experience thus assisting with the design and manage an aspect of the tourism product. Pine and Gilmore's (1999) '4E model of experience realms and their staging experiences model', helps to identify the four types of experiences sought by the customer, and also suggests how to stage such experiences at a destination.

Staging the Experience Economy:

	Passive Participation	Active Participation
Absorption	Experience: Entertainment Engagement by performances, talks, music or dance recitals, discourses. Innovation: Waiters to be performing artist as the tourist consumes both the food and the performance	Experience: Education Enhancement of Knowledge and skills Innovation: A tourist travelling from USA to Goa, India to learn the traditional 'Dodol' and ' Belseza' (Two Variants of Wheat Pudding) making on open flame
Involvement	Experience: Esthetic (Aesthetic in other texts) Sensual enrichment through the environment Innovation: An underwater museum where the tourist has to walk on the sea bed to experience both the marine life and artefacts.	Experience: Escapism Gets engrossed in space and time Innovation: Past life regression session on a mountain top, or a museum providing spa services in a tree house

Source: Author, 2022

Getting it together with a destination profile

The models discussed in the previous chapter will be useless unless tied to sustainable development goals. While it is also important to profile a destination to know all about the place. Starting from the host and their behavior, the geographic location, the traditional knowledge available in the destination, the experiences that can be generated, provisions for zoning if available. The typology of tourists who will be willing to experience this location. The generating area and transit areas. The TALC stage of the destination. Prioritizing the SDG 2030 for the tourism area. The provisions for calculation of multipliers to measure the economic impact and carrying capacity to identify the environmental impact of tourism at that location.

View a sample destination profile here:

http://online.fliphtml5.com/kordh/avnq

http://online.fliphtml5.com/feptb/wgps/

http://online.fliphtml5.com/feptb/bpye/

2 INNOVATION AND SUSTAINABILITY

About the chapter:

Innovation can generate curiosity among tourist and a good story told about a destination can ensure the much-needed tourist and audience, who are ready to experience tourism and make it memorable. Techniques to think out of the box is an essential skill that makes a manager valuable in a world of disruptions. Tourism based innovations from around the world are also discussed which can inspire readers to implement similar ideas in their start-ups or businesses.

Chapter entails:

> Why innovate?
> Types of innovation, what's best for me?
> Thinking out of the box (Known to Unknown)
> Innovations that inspire.
  - Key learning points
  - Facilitators checkpoint
  - Managerial implications

Why Innovate?

Tourist is always on the lookout for something new, a new story to tell back home or to friends. The local experiences blended with innovation will add value to a destination visited. Destination managers have to remember that a fresh perspective and tourist gaze are very important to promote a tourism product. Innovation can be either an extension of traditional knowledge or of information technology in the delivery of tourism services. Innovation can have a long term effect, in some instances, it can forge new partnerships and establish linkages between stakeholders through strong networking capabilities. On the flipside, it can also lead to disruptions in existing systems and make existing procedures redundant and call for a new installation and change. It is the destination managers' onus to identify what type of innovation can conserve the local beliefs and networks than cause sudden disruptions in a tourist region. To illustrate an act of disruption due to innovation: a traditional wind-mill used to grind wheat getting replaced by the modern wind-mill to produce energy, with an assumption that additional energy produced can also be utilised to power an electric mill. However the novelty that a tourist gets while visiting the heritage building will be lost and has to be conserved by the efforts of both the residents and the destination manager. To illustrate how a traditional structure can apply innovative techniques to promote tourism. Himachal Pradesh, in India is a land blessed with waterfalls, traditional wind-mills are indigenously built over small waterfalls and a local entrepreneur converting this mill into a home-stay is an innovative method to provide novelty to the tourist.

Types of innovation, what's best for me?

A destination manager has to apply due diligence while adopting innovations in tourism. It's important to understand the vision, mission, and objectives of your organisation and then align with the innovation that is a best fit. This chapter will discuss about innovations in tourism and ideas that are prevalent even during the pandemic making travel touch less, green, and contributing to economic growth of the local community. Some of the best models of innovation are:

Green Innovation Models

With an intent to protect the environment, tourism businesses introduced innovations that uses renewable resources. These include, but and are not limited to the reuse of towels, energy-efficient lighting, packed lunches and beverages with steel tiffin boxes and bottles that need to be returned to the pantry, protection of soil from erosion by using locally available products, efficiency in the recycling of kitchen and general waste, grey water, and composting, rain-water harvesting, solar energy for cooking, lighting, and heating. Apart from this the residents become beneficiaries through employment opportunities and sharing of their traditional knowledge with the guest through story telling methods.

Abernathy and Clark Model for Innovation

This model proposed four types of innovation namely; Regular, Niche, Revolutionary, and Architectural Innovations. If you look at these concepts in through a Johari window you will notice the culmination of two concepts can result in the conservation of existing competencies and linkages, while a merger of the other two concepts can have a disruptive outcome on competencies and linkages.

Illustration of Abernathy and Clark Model for Innovation

	Disrupt Existing Competence	Conservation of Existing Competence
Conserve Existing Linkages	**Revolutionary Innovations** • New technology is diffused into business firms • Introduction of methods that change the staff composition • Same market penetration with new methods	**Regular Innovations** • Promotion of new investments to increase productivity • Training of proprietors and staff to operate more efficiently • Incremental rise in quality and standards
Disrupt or Create New Linkages	**Architectural Innovations** • Creation of new events and attractions that demand reorganisation. • Redefining the physical or legal infrastructure • Creating centres of excellence that treat and disseminate new operational research based knowledge.	**Niche Innovations** • Promote the entry of new entrepreneurs to exploit business opportunities • Encourage firms to enter new marketing alliances • Combine existing products in new ways

Source: Author re-created from the basic Abernathy and Clark Model for Innovation for tourism, 2022

Innovations can promote knowledge transfer and knowhow to the local business of tourism. A destination manager has to decide what would be the best way forward based on the four types of innovations suitable for tourism. There are four systems that enable transfer of knowledge to the tourism business, they are: The trade system, the infrastructure system, the regulation system, and the technological system. The trade system governs aspects such as administration of market surveys and analysis, best practices, certifications, and standards. The technological system focuses on development of equipment and technology, production, and outsourcing. The infrastructural system is linked to natural and cultural attractions, traffic and transportation. The regulation system is associated with control of safety standards, economic control, environmental systems, and labour regulations.

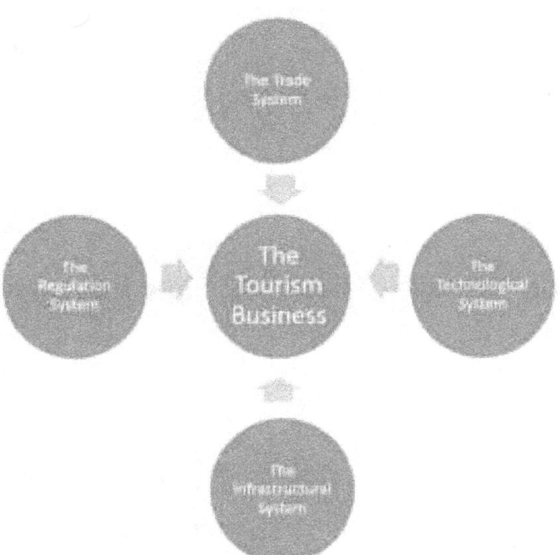

Source: Author re-created from Anne, Pergamons knowledge transfer channels to the tourism business

Business model innovation

Due to the rising cost of fuel and maintenance costs, airlines introduced the hub and spoke concept business model. This is observed in airlines such as Qatar Airways, they depend on the feeder cities or airports and gather passengers to a central point also known as the hub and then distribute the passengers to the final destination. This type of model ensures that the flights are always optimally utilised. As it is known that the tourism product is highly perishable and a vacant seat means loss of revenue for that flight. An innovation that was introduced by Captain Gopinath of Air Deccan, was to price all the flights across India to a Rs. 500/- per sector. And to overcome the loss of revenue, he also introduced Rs. 1/- flight. When questioned about why he offered to sell a seat at a dirt-cheap price, he would say that he is giving a flying experience to a person who has never flown before and at the same time dignity of purchasing a flight ticket. These Rs. 1/- tickets were a hit among the Indian consumers and the airline gained popularity due to its innovative ideas. Another innovation in the airline industry was to hedge the fuel cost for five years so that the price fluctuations and inflation would not disrupt its flight operations, this was introduced by Mr. Herb Kelleher, CEO of South West Airlines till his death in 2019, The concept of Low-Cost Carrier (LCC) became a new business model and was embraced by many carriers across the world, the other name for LCC is the no-frills carrier. All on-board amenities such as meals, blankets, entertainment, beverages, soft drinks, snacks, and water were unbundled from the full fare of the ticket and the passenger could choose to purchase these on-board the flight if required.

Levels of Innovation:

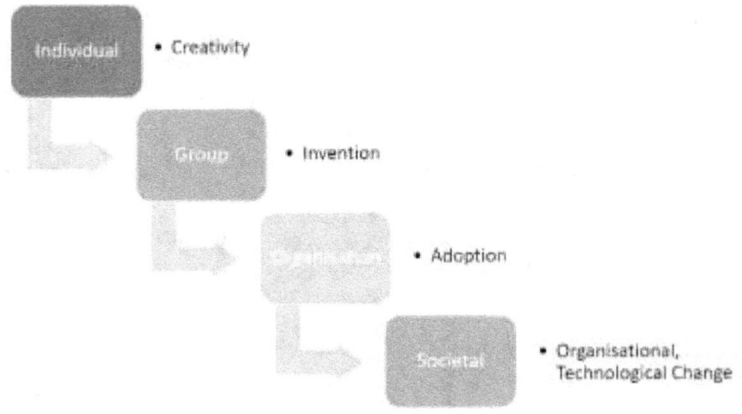

Source: Author, 2022

Individual, Group, Organisation and Societal Innovation.

The building block for societal innovation is through the individual innovation, the factors that motivate an individual is the given task and the psychological empowerment. While the resources in task domain is associated with work experience, knowledge of the job, expertise and cognitive aptitude. Innovation management skills such as creative cognitive style, biographical history and personality. The next level is the group innovation here the motivation to innovate comes from the team climate, leader member exchange and group norms. The resources in task domain is effected by team-member exchange or organisation citizenship behaviour, group functional or demographic diversity, group size and resource slack. Innovation management skills are participative management, power, commitment, support of innovation, champion or group leader, informational or constructive conflict, boundary roles or gatekeepers. Organisational innovation is linked to the motivation that is brought about by organisation vision or strategy, climate for implementation, innovation attribute or management-decision variables. Resource in task domain is absorptive capacity, complex division of labour, managerial professionalism or cosmopolitanism. While innovation management skills are ability to manage conflict, resistance to change, synchronous adoption of different innovation types, knowledge management, and corporate entrepreneurship. Societal innovation which displays the all-round innovation to the tourist has the motivating factor due to market demand, opportunities, global competitiveness, technological dynamism, societal, culture and demography. Under resource and task domain we have the human or social capital, labour productivity, information infrastructure. The Innovation management skills are government stimuli and collaborative initiatives.

Innovations in travel technological domains are:

- Email

- Development of applications (apps)

- Aviation

- Social Media

- Global Distribution Systems (GDS)

- Virtual Reality(VR)

- Translations of sound and light show narratives

- Artificial Intelligence (AI)

- Digitisation of currency (Crypto currency)

Thinking out of the box

What it means to think out of a box

When a destination manager intends to innovate, the concept of thinking out of the box can be adopted. We all live in our box, our comfort zone, and bringing us out of this zone can become a little unsettling. Thinking out of the box involves such radical thinking or thought process that sometimes can be absurd, risky, and ridiculous. The reason why innovations work is because of their novelty in delivering a tourism experience, novelty is one of the major constructs that make a tourism experience memorable at the destination. So if innovations are structured in such a manner that they can provide novelty to the end-user it can become successful. Thinking out of the box can be applied to a business problem, it can be done in form of a brainstorming activity, and it's advisable to use the mind-map template, where the central question or problem lies inside the box, is solved by solutions from outside the box. Moving from the known to the unknown is the key.

Steps to think out of the box

A study conducted by Forbes suggests that ability to think creatively and without stress also depends on your Emotional Quotient (EQ) and Personality type both Interpersonal skills and Intrapersonal skills are a strength and people need to identify their strength and work towards its empowerment. Brainstorming can be done as a group activity if you have a team or as an individual. If you are a creative tourism writer trying to attract tourists to a destination. Writing all types of ideas around the central problem is the best way to go forward, and while doing so you need to keep your mind free from biases that can crop up. At this level it is important not to shoot down any ideas due to its novelty or because it was never done before. Even if it means that path is going in a different tangent altogether. By doing this the boundaries set in your mind are broken and the walls of the box, your comfort zone are broken.

At this stage re-engineering or re-conceptualizing, your problem is very important. You can now solve your problem using these three steps:

Step 1 turn the image upside down. Humans recognise patterns and attribute meaning to it. For example a triangle is associated with a pyramid or a mountain. So if we turn this image upside down it challenges the human mind towards its novelty and structure. Humans tend to think of things in a particular fashion or swearing by the policy method. When you turn the image upside down you focus on the geometric pattern than what your biased mind thinks about a pattern.

Step 2 working backward towards a problem is a sure-shot way to come up with a solution, think about the ideal situation, and what it takes to keep it in the ideal situation. This method is also used in reverse engineering, and helps to identify loopholes and short comings in a process or system.

Step 3 change your central theme and focus on ideas that have come up on your mind map and how they can serve as a step forward. Sometimes even after tying these methods you may still hit a roadblock some ways to overcome these would be to surround yourself with people who have innovative ideas, study other industries, try to learn something new. Think of ways in which mundane things can be used to become purposeful, for example in a rural tourism area, where the bullock cart is no longer in use it can be used as a centerpiece in a lawn that can be painted and decorated for the tourist to view.

You are a destination manager at a place that houses a heritage monument a wind-mill, that still waters the garden, and this facility is run by a family that still grinds the wheat at this spot. List all the possible ideas that you can think of to make a tourist visit to this place a memorable one.

Innovations that inspire.

The tourism industry has become highly innovative some creative innovations are presented in the way experiences are designed while in other cases it depends on how technology drives the future of tourism. The pandemic has impacted the tourism industry tremendously and made the service providers come up with innovations to serve the travel customer. The hospitality industry has realised the importance of touch less services. The accommodation sector now has introduced face recognition which allows the customer to check-in without interacting with the front office staff.

VR Goggles:

Image credit: pixabay.com

Virtual tours of the cities to be visited on a tour gives a 360 degree experience of how the place looks like even before visiting the destination. Apps such as **timelooper** can take you back in time around 750 years and experience the place in its historical splendour. Airlines such as Lufthansa also gives its future customer a feel of how their inflight services feel like even to the extent of pouring wine into the glasses, by the use virtual reality head gear. Interaction with artificial intelligence, also reduces the impact of errors that are done during human interactions.

The Hyper loop:

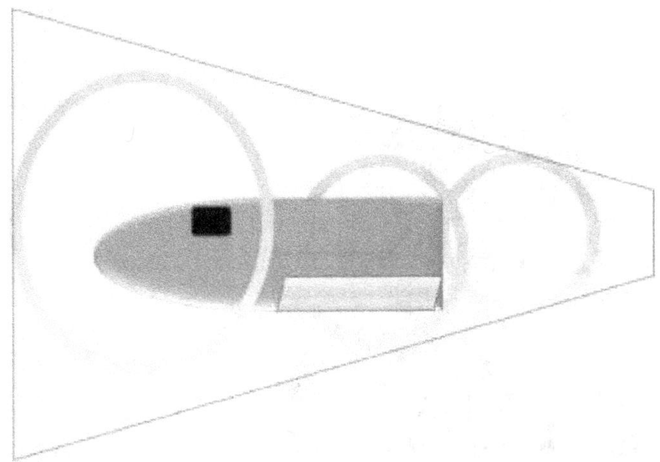

Source: Author, 2022

This is the most efficient manner of travel with minimum impact to the environment. The system uses electric propulsion and can accelerate passenger or cargo vehicle through a tube in a low pressure environment. Some of the benefits is saving of time, on-demand travel, less emissions, can eliminate human error, environment friendly and faster than air travel which is its plus point.

It was introduced in 2016 and tested on a one mile stretch in Nevada. The hyper loop is a technological innovation that leverages time taken for travel. It is also considered to be a safe mode of transportation. The current plans are to develop a hyper loop between San Francisco and Los Angeles, which is a 350 mile distance from each other and will take 35 minutes for travel between the two points. Competitively a flight takes 1 hour and 30 minutes, while travel by car without traffic should take around 5 hours and 40 minutes.

Digital Currency

Image credit: pixabay.com

BitCoin ATM's: Now travelers can enjoy a destination without a worry about carrying plastic money, converting or exchanging money, carrying traveller's cheques as some countries have made the virtual currency a reality. Biometrics would be sufficient to conduct the transactions and payments, which is the way forward for tourist who need not bother about carrying cash in their wallets.

Smart Rentals

Image credit: pixabay.com

Rent-a-gear: Travellers now do not have to pay for the extra luggage of bikes, surfboard or ski gear anymore as owners at the destination can now list their gear and the tourist can rent them out for the duration of the stay.

Send-Bags-Ahead:

Image credit: pixabay.com

This can save up time related to check-in and check-out process, where the bags are handled by professional handlers who would charge fraction of the cost that you would pay as ancillary fees to the airlines. It is an efficient way of transporting luggage especially for accessible or silver tourist. One of the best example is mybaggage.

 A destination manager has a plethora of innovation models to choose from, the best fit would be the one that blends into the destination that is being managed. A tourist can experience an eco-tourism destination in advance before deciding to purchase the tour package. Elimination, disruption or mergers of existing linkages and competencies, can assist the destination manager to design innovations. If customers are also made to partake in the design of the destination, such inputs can also make it more successful to co-create innovations. Technology has assisted the travel industry tremendously and the innovations continue to unfold making travel more efficient. Innovations can reduce time, cost and can lower the negative impact on environment which is a priority for a sustainable destination.

3 SUSTAINABLE TOURISM POLICY

About the Chapter:

A concept is incomplete without the grounded theories linked to it, which gives us the direction for the development of future policies. Buy-in from stakeholders is as important while planning to develop a tourism policy. Without such handshakes, it is possible for tourism policies to gather dust in the policy dossier folders without anyone taking it further. Once the preliminary stages are fulfilled it is easy to scale the advanced stages of policymaking and ensure that it is implemented. Fortunately, the SDG 2030 has given a direction to the tourism industry to include such changes in its operations. Learning from the best in the industry also can inspire others to innovate in their localized systems.

Chapter entails:

> Associated grounded theories
> Inclusiveness in policymaking
> Stages of policy building and implementation
> Case study of sustainable tourism policies
  - Key learning points
  - Facilitators checkpoint
  - Managerial implications

Grounded theories of tourism policy making

It's imperative to understand what a grounded theory is and is not. The premise of a grounded theory is to gain insight and construct knowledge about a phenomenon. While it is not based on a pre-conceived notion so a researcher should not include their biases into the theory that is developed. In the word of Charmaz (2011) it is 'an iterative, comparative, interactive, and abductive method', that being said it is also not about developing an universal law but to develop fresh insights about a phenomenon and facilitate in building a new theory (Matteucci and Gnoth, 2017). These are some of the famous grounded theories with a brief understanding of each: Classical Grounded Theory is a method of theory generation than employing analytical methods this was founded by Glaser and Strauss in 1967, The Modified Strauss was introduced in 1990 by Strauss and Corbin, it is systematic in nature as it involves three step process of coding which are inductive, axial and selective. It allows flexible interpretation of the researcher and the qualitative data that is collected for this purpose. While Constructivist theory is based on the researchers own understanding of society and reality. Feminist theory is derived from the nursing discipline and is based on multiple interpretation of reality while examining diversity, privilege and power-relations. Post-modern theory is based on mapping the social world and identification of aspects that are left unsaid (Turner, 2016).

For the purpose of this book as grounded theory is not that restrictive and allows for pluralism. We will proceed with the theory of Constructivist and Post-modern theory as tourism is majorly focused on society, social innovations, co-creation and interactions of the social world. Also a facet of Modified Strauss theory also applies to qualitative data studies of tourism. Tourism policy is not an independent and interpretative outcome of a select or privileged few who are at the seat of power. Implementation of the grounded theory comes in the forefront to solve societal problems, ideally associated with climate change, environmental issues, unemployment and imbalance in economic status of countries and the resident population. For a tourism policy to be developed an inclusive method has to be employed firstly by adopting qualitative methods of data gathering the methods may include, transcripts of interviews (ideally signed by the participants with their consent), audio, video recordings, and pictorial representations. Further coding of the data and re-coding them into meaningful interpretations that are based on social-realities will enable policy makers to develop a sound policy for tourism.

Defining Tourism Policy

Among the myriads of definition of tourism policy the most authoritative narrative is provided by Goeldner and Ritchie and reproduced verbatim:

> 'Tourism policy can be defined as a set of regulations, rules, guidelines, directives, and development / promotion objectives and strategies that provide a framework within which the collective and individual decisions directly affecting long - term tourism development and the daily activities within a destination are taken.'

While UNWTO has further cautioned what the policies should be associated with while being administered at a tourism destination. This guideline provided during the UNWTO Framework Convention on Tourism Ethics held in 2020 states that:

> Tourism policies and activities should be conducted with respect for the artistic, archaeological and cultural heritage, which they should protect and pass on to future generations; particular care should be devoted to preserving monuments, worship sites, archaeological and historic sites as well as upgrading museums which must be widely open and accessible to tourism visits.

Inclusiveness in policymaking

From the two definitions it is clear that a frame-work has to be built, while emphasis was laid on collective and individual decision making process. While the UNWTO framework provided more clarity as to what has to be preserved and for whom. Terms such as care and upgrade call for further opportunities of employment and social gain for residents of a destination while also promoting education and skill building in the up-keep of heritage and tourism assets.

This also poses a question as to who are the actors involved in developing the tourism policy and from where the inputs have to be derived. The focus should be on minimising negative impacts and maximising the benefits to the destination and its dwellers.

Quick Reference Grid:

Intrinsic Involvement	Residents or host			
Stakeholder Involvement	Local	Regional	Provincial	National
Government	X	X	X	X
Environmental Groups	X	X	-	X
Visitors/excursionists	X	-	-	-
Tourism Industry Sectors	X	X	-	X
Destination Management Organisation (DMO's)	X	X	-	X
Cultural/heritage groups	X	X	-	X
Social/health and Educational groups	X	X	-	X
Extrinsic Involvement	Remote visitors and tourist			

Source: Author, 2022

Stages of policy building

The tourism policy formulation may involve a similar approach used in design methodology or quality management.

Step 1: A modified design centric approach used PADDIE method to develop a new policy.

Step 2: DMAIC principle can be adopted to maintain the quality of the policy document.

It is imperative that before setting out into these methods the philosophies, vision, mission and objectives of the destination has to be well defined.

Design centric approach or the PADDIE method.

The fulfilment of each stage kick-off the beginning of the next stage and has to be repeated for a constant upgrade to the existing policy that is made.

Stage 1: Planning, without including the policy making process in the planning of a destination it may not be very well received by the intrinsic stakeholders who are the 'host'. They have to be well informed and involved in the planning phase and should involve themselves throughout the stages of design of the policy. It is a well favoured thought to outsource such work to experts, and little contribution is sought from the 'host'. This approach or attitude can create a conflict resulting in rejection of a well thought of plan for implementation. Dialogue has to be initiated at this stage and the data collection is the binding force between the stages of planning and analysis.

Stage 2: Analysis can happen at both internal and external levels. While internal analysis examines the existing tourism policy if any and reviews it for further development. For a completely new policy structure, where external analysis is mandated, this is the stage where the grounded theories kick in and where most of the ground work is involved in terms of coding and interpretation of the data collected through geo-spatial tracking, interviews – written, verbal or video graphed, and data associated with tourism demand and supply. The entire data has to be analysed by employing the Modified Straussian method of inductive, axial and selective process and other quantitative processes where applicable.

Stage 3: Design, at this stage the narrative of the policy has to be written down, by the inputs received from the stage 2. This stage builds the framework of the destinations tourism policy, which should include all the aspects such as socio, economic and political fabric of that society, this stage should also focus on the regulations associated with the up-keep of the destination. Rules, regulations, directives and marketing opportunities should be included at this stage that provides a guiding beacon to all the stakeholders of the destination.

Stage 4: Develop, The policy document should be wetted out at this stage and the proper signoffs from all the major stakeholders should be received, this stage should follow a democratic approach by including all the stakeholders and their representatives.

Stage 5: Implement, The policy document should now become a legal reality with endorsement at a government level and enforcers should be also given authority to take decisions with regard to non-compliance of the documented policy. The enforcers are the local, municipal, provincial or state and national governing bodies along with the judiciary and the law enforces. Implementation stage should also involve educating the arriving tourist about their need to comply and having a fruitful tourism experience in the destination.

Stage 6: Evaluation, this stage should be conducted on a regular basis as there can be chances of diverting back to old systems or getting into a state of inertia due to lack of participation or lacklustre compliance from the authorities. The process has to be kept active and has to be revisited on a half yearly and yearly basis to further improve the policy document. The complete modification has to be done every decade in order to have a fully functional and active tourism policy document.

Step 2: DMAIC ideally used in quality control of systems and processes can also be employed at the evaluation stage. Here involvement of researchers, existing quantitative data from the tourism arrivals, tourist experiences, multipliers and other point of contacts can be gathered through big-data analysis. At this step automation also can be employed along with artificial intelligence interventions. The steps involved are: **define** which can be gathered from the pre-planning step, followed by **measure** which is completely data driven and can be **analysed** further to be interpreted into meaningful information, **improvement** of procedures as in simplification of processes involved in receiving tourist, regulatory matters and managing their entry and exit formalities may be further improved, **control** also calls for enforcement and containing issues such as ill-effects of mass-tourism, over-tourism, issues such as illegal and un-regulated growth in sensitive destinations.

Case studies of sustainable tourism policies: Pro's and Con's

Case Study of Thailand's '7 Greens Sustainable Tourism Policy' at Koi Samui is the best example for the policy design process which as beautifully designed with maximum involvement of the stakeholders. Thailand follows a three tier government system i.e. Local, State and National. Tourism Authority of Thailand (TAT) introduced the policy in 2008 and aligned it with the National Tourism Policy of 2012-16, the policy document received a lot of awards way in advance as it was not yet implemented across Thailand, but only to four areas in Thailand. The plan was ambitious as the vision spoke about distribution of tourism benefits with locals in a sustainable way. On the other hand the seven greens had based its concepts as: tourist responsibility towards environment, environment friendly modes of transportation, promotion of green destination, support of local communities, promotion of tourism activities that suit local communities, positive first impression for visitors while demonstrating respect, care and concern for the environment, encouragement of corporate social responsibility among operators and promote use and development of renewable energy sources. The ABC method of implementation was adopted by the consultants, wherein A stands for Advocacy and Acceptance, B for Benchmarking and C for Carry forward. The implementation of the 7 Greens policy took effect from May –September 2012 with the three stage approach followed by the consultants namely assessment of environmental and cultural impacts, 'Umbrella' partners included trade associations, local government, national government, Non-government organisations (NGOs) and community groups. 430 tourism stake holders were invited in which 306 were other 'tourism related businesses', the response was from 145 stakeholders which increased to 430 gradually. A set of 20 Indicators of rudimentary sustainable practices were identified and a compilation of pre and post Policy implementation buy-in incremental changes were recorded.

Some of the negative impacts were also recorded post the implementation of the policy though Koi Samui was the most successful among rest of the destinations, however it was not without criticism there was a lack of buy-in from local communities, local governments and non-tourism related bodies even after the challenging task taken up by the consultants throughout the project implementation and delivery stages. Three years down the line after initiation of the famed 7 Greens; William of Paddle Asia, a Nature and adventure-based operator who was of the opinion that 'Historically the TAT talks about sustainable tourism and eco-tourism, and has a few conferences – usually in very un eco-friendly mega resorts – and hands out eco awards mostly to mass tourism companies that have nothing to do with low impact tourism,'. The destination Koi Samui had already reached its optimal tourism life cycle stage and was on the verge of decline due to the ecological and social impacts of tourism which was related to degradation of beaches, challenges of garbage treatment, proliferating hotels, ecological imbalances due to sand and gravel mining, and inaccessible beach areas to the locals. There was an increase in massage parlours, bars and prostitution.

A 360 degree review method was used to identify as to why the implementation stage was weak at Koi Samui which was one of the pilot case among the four regions selected for the '7Greens' policy implementation. In their findings they termed it as 'feel good-do little' policy, the initial enthusiasm was high, and later the support of stakeholders declined. Objectives were unclear, and long term commitment towards implementation and focus was lacking. Crony capitalism in terms of low-level and high-level corruption existed. Bureaucrats were unwilling to support initiatives that would weaken their political influence (Muangasame and McKercher, 2014). Lessons from the 7 Greens policy, though the policy document itself embodies aspects from Global Code of Ethics for Tourism and also has SDG concepts imbibed in it though the SDG's 17 concepts were not yet formulated till 2017. What happened to the ambitious plan of sharing of wealth with the stakeholders in Thailand is still not known. This could be the major reason for fall-out of the stakeholders of tourism.

Questions:

1. From the above case study identify the stakeholder involvement in the design of 7 greens policy.
2. What are the high-points of the 7 greens policy stages?
3. What went wrong with the 7 greens policy and how will you as a policy maker or destination manager can overcome such challenges at your destination?
4. Use the problem, cause and solutions method to suggest how this issue can be managed better.

Managerial implication:

 Policy formulation and implementation is an inclusive process, and can decay at a very alarming rate if there are changes in the governmental reigns or sudden political decisions that abandon older policies. Some of the well-designed polices can tend to suffer if it is not properly factored into the constitution of a country. A country aligned to the sustainable development goals, also can utilize the 17 goals as a guiding beacon to design its tourism policy. Among the 17 SGD's the ones that were earmarked by UNWTO through their internal assessment were SDG 8, 12, 17. Where SDG 8 speaks about the **goal of decent work and economic growth**; tourism being a driver for growth can contribute towards this goal and skilling the residents can generate income generating opportunities as an entrepreneur or as an employee of a tourism based organisation. While SDG 12 focuses on **Sustainable Consumption and Production**, both these factors should take into consideration the strain on the environment due to excessive and unregulated tourism, and over tourism, the needs of the

local population and the supply for the visitors and tourist. All the methods adopted here should have renewable sources of energy for consumption as well as production as required by the tourism industry. At the level of SDG 17, **Partnerships for the Goals** is emphasised and requires strong diplomatic ties between participating countries which can promote knowledge exchange and further research and development by collaborating with an advanced nation.

Facilitator can refer the learners to further research on best practices associated with tourism policy development which includes inclusiveness, and the 5A's of an effective destination. The learners can also be given instruction on drafting a tourism policy to revive a destination that has reached the saturation stage on its TALC graph.

4 SUSTAINABLE TOURISM PLANNING

About the Chapter:

Identification of persons who signoff and stakeholders who need to be involved, is an essential step before planning. This chapter will take the learner step by step through all the nuances that can be easily missed out. It will follow a mind-mapping technique to cover all the elements. Some techniques such as effective project planning will also be shared to ensure an end-to-end view of the planning stages. Planning is incomplete without implementation, as part of a project management process pilot, beta testing by implementation will also be discussed. The entire section will culminate by measuring the success of the plan that was implemented. Return on investment (ROI) will be tied to the triple bottom line.

Chapter Entails:

> Basics of sustainable tourism planning(STP)
> Stake holders involved in the STP process
> Stages of the STP process
> Implementing an STP
> Measuring the success
>> Key learning points
>> Facilitators checkpoint
>> Managerial implications

Basics of sustainable tourism planning (STP)

Policy formulation precedes sustainable tourism planning, and every tourist destination needs a plan that will ensure that the area is well managed. The policy should clearly state the goals and objectives that are associated with the plan. Plants are not myopic and should have a future focus ideally, five, ten, fifty to a hundred years in future. That calls for a collective brain work and identification of every constraint that can make a plan to fail. Tourism is most sought after industry among developing nations as it can improve the socio-economic conditions of a destination. However it comes with a caveat that it is not a plug and play solution and can also carry its own baggage of problems. A very thorough consideration is required to first understand the cost and benefits of implementing tourism activities in a destination. If the cost outweigh its benefits then it can do more harm to the destination. Therefore a good plan can provide a vision, and socio-economic goals for the areas where tourism growth is proposed, it also provides for a road-map ahead of the long journey.

The purpose of development of a good plan are for these basic reasons.

1. Organisation Development

2. Community Involvement

3. Tourism Product Development

4. Tourism Product Marketing

With these core purposes in consideration, it is now important to ask some questions that will assist in the planning process.

Question 1: Where are we now?

Question 2: Where do we want to be in one, five and ten years?

Question 3: How do we get there? or How do we achieve this?

Question 4: How did we do? (Results may be positive or need further improvement)

Definitions of Planning

A well framed definition can guide its readers towards the actions which can be implemented. Some of the well-known definitions are:

Planning is concerned with anticipating and regulating change in a system to promote orderly development so as to increase the social, economic and environmental benefits of the development process. To do this, planning becomes 'an ordered sequence of operations, designed to lead to the achievement of either a single goal or to a balance between several goals' (Murphy 1985, p.156).

According to Gunn (1994) the focus of planning is mainly to generate income and employment, and ensure resource conservation and traveller satisfaction. The definition further clarifies that under-developed destinations can received guidelines for further development.

Spanoudis (1982) proposed that, Tourism planning must always proceed within the framework of an overall plan for the development of an area's total resources; and local conditions and demands must be satisfied before any other considerations are met (p.314).

Types of Plan:

As destination mangers it is also essential to understand what plan would best suit the destination, baseline evaluation of whether it is a developed, developing or under-developed destination has to be first done. Selection of the type of plan applicable for the selected destination would be the second step. The four major types of planning which can help in attainment of the short and long term goals are strategic, tactical, operational, and contingency (Basnyat, 2021). Plans that follow a top down approach is termed as strategic plan, the idea is to include the destinations mission, vision, values and goals. These plans are ideally spread over a longer duration of three to ten years. They steer the important decisions to be taken during its term. As a successor of the strategic plan, the tactical plan is more oriented towards 'how' to accomplish the mission associated with destination development. The tactical plan are flexible in nature and break the strategy into small actionable parts. While the operational plans are executable on a short-run, they can be ongoing or for single-use, they can be associated with implementation of a campaign, they can entail regulations and daily operations of the destination. Tourism has its highs and lows, there are always surprises in terms of natural calamities, disasters, pandemics, epidemics which is always looming over a destination. Factoring these unseen changes and getting out of the state of inertia or 'status-quo' is very important, to assist with this need the contingency plan is a must for every destination.

Planning – Pro's and Cons

A destination manager has to know how a bad planning can negatively impact a destination. Some of these occur due to overtourism and revenge tourism that causes a mass influx of tourist if the destination is not well regulated. This results in overcrowding, negative customer experience. Commodification of local culture, loss of cultural identity, inflation and unreasonable increase in cost of living in the destination.

While a well thought plan can help heal a destination, improve its image and create memorable tourism experiences in the minds of the visitors and tourist. The residents can benefit from entrepreneurship and employment opportunities due to a positive tourism stimulus, quality of living improves, development of infrastructure happens in a phased manner, and clear guidelines are provided for preservation of culture, heritage and natural resources.

Stake holders involved in STP

Group dynamics holds a pivotal role during the STP process. There are multiple actors and stake holders who contribute towards the planning process. While some of the higher level personnel may provide their inputs at the policy level, they may be directly or indirectly involved in the planning stage.

Hierarchy of the stake holders in STP

Tier	Stake holders	Strata
1	[illegible]	[illegible]
2	[illegible]	[illegible]
3	[illegible]	[illegible]
4	[illegible]	[illegible]
5	[illegible]	[illegible]
6	[illegible]	[illegible]
7	[illegible]	[illegible]
8	[illegible]	[illegible]
9	[illegible]	[illegible]

Source: Recreated from the Stakeholders and roles in sustainable tourism by Author, 2022

The above table clearly depicts the involvement of multiple levels of stake holders that can help make a destination tourism policy implementable. Due to the multi-level involvement of such stake holders it gets cumbersome to involve everyone in the planning stage, a work around in terms of clusters will help and Delphi technique can be used to gather inputs from all the levels of the stake holders if it is not possible to get everyone on the same platform. The results of these discussions can be further analysed using appropriate software through the method of thematic analysis to derive a pattern of responses from the participants.

The role of the stake holder in the STP process.

There are nine tiers of stake holders who will in some way influence the manner in which a destination is developed. Leaving out even one layer can cause disruption and friction which are difficult to manager at a later stage of implementation. The role of each tier of the STP process are:

Tier 1: International development assistance agencies

Their role is more of directive in nature and there is low involvement in the actual planning process. Due to their proximity to the decision making authorities, their major role is to ensure that tourism is integrated in development policies and agreements. They are also a catalyst to provide financial and technical assistance to sustainable tourism projects and programmes.

Tier 2: National Government

This layer is also majorly directive and they are the drivers of the planning process and have direct involvement with the implementers of the planning stage. Their role is inclined towards strategy development and implementation, associating sustainable tourism sector projects to policies, strategies, legislations, standards, and regulations. They are involved in planning the resources, infrastructure and its development at the destination. Due to their access to tourism budget and branding they are intensively involved in communication, information sharing and marketing of the destination.

Tier 3: Local Government and destination bodies

These stake holders are the implementers and their function is to provide local strategic direction and planning, they implement the policy and regulations provided by Tier 2 stake holders. Directly involved in developing the local infrastructure and its management.

They can further involve the Tier 4 stake holders through active engagement, coordination and support.

Tier 4: Private sector businesses

They are the key players who mobilise the entire planning process in tourism as they are the doer's of the policy that is set by the higher tier levels. Their major involvement is through representation of the sector, influence on the tourism sector. They carry out the operations of the tourism services, they also have a direct link to domestic and international markets. They develop products through investment and improvement. Their prominent role is to generate employment and contribute in the increase of local income. Their very strongly involved in the development and operations process that affect the triple bottom line.

Tier 5: Employees and related bodies

This layer is directly involved with the social aspect of the sustainable tourism planning process. Representation is done in the interest of the entire body of employees, it also involves planning and development of the human resources than the destination itself through skill development and education. They are expected to provide quality and reliable service in return for income.

Tier 6: NGOs – International, national and local

These have stake holder representation from every tier of the STP process. They represent the stake holder interests, they are involved in strategic planning and development, stake holder coordination and supporting implementation. Their major contribution is through capacity building and provision of expertise.

Tier 7: Education and training bodies

Their role is similar to the tier 6 level, however they are also involved in knowledge assimilation and dissemination. They provide a tactical support to the policy developed and strategy to implement such policies. They are also involved in capacity building and training in collaboration with the tier 6 strata, and can also provide specific advice and expertise.

Tier 8: Local community

This strata is involved in planning and decision making which is related at a local level. They represent the local community and communicate their interest to the higher tiers. They negotiate for equitable benefit sharing among the community, they interact with the tourist to benefit mutually, and they receive income from tourist spending as they are the direct beneficiary of the multiplier effect.

Tier 9: Consumers/tourists

They become the major source of income to the tourism sector. They are expected to behave responsibly towards the environment and local communities, through their travel choices and actions. They are also involved in sharing of accurate and fair information and opinion about the destination visited.

Stages of the STP process

As part of the STP process a destination manager should follow the SMART Technique to formulate objectives while planning for the development of a destination.

Let us examine the SMART approach in assessment of an objectives specified in Example 1-3

Example 1: The human resource income from tourist consumption of tourism products and services should increase by 3% annually over the next five years.

Example 2: Increase in the average cultural knowledge of visitors by 50% within five years.

Example 3: Provide a memorable tourism experience to 4000 tourist that arrive annually at this wild-life sanctuary.

Specific:

Clarity of vision is very important so that all the stakeholders agree to the objective. They should be clear with the meaning and take onus of their role in achieving the objective.

Inference, in example 1, the time frame of five years indicate it is a long term plan, the incremental approach towards income on an annual basis also indicates that there will be human resource development to maintain the service quality and reliability and enable the labour force to claim such an increase. This is directly associated with Tier 5: Employees and related bodies

Measurable:

If the planning objective is measurable it provides a basis towards progress evaluation. Destination managers will be able to assess, determine and decide on the allocation of efforts to achieve this objective in future. It also provides the elements of the destination that require monitoring and its frequency.

Inference, the example 1 also identifies that human resources income has to be measured and it should confirm to the percentage that was determined at its inception, while all due diligence should be taken to ensure that this measurement takes place on a yearly basis till the maturity of the objective which is five years.

Achievable:

The objectives should be realistic and doable as per the set time frame, the implementer should be able to achieve the outcome with the available funding and resources. For a destination manager it provides a motivation for further action and to the other stake holders it gives a sense of future accomplishment. The focus should be on the desired goal than the one than the situation they are currently in.

Inference: The example 2 gives a long term plan for five years, while the focus is on co-creation and learning by involving the visitors in the cultural immersion programme there by increasing their knowledge from their present state to 50%.

Results Oriented:

The objectives deal with results or accomplishment of a specified activity. It gives the destination manager what has to be achieved but 'how to' is left to the manager's creativity.

Inference: Example 3 gives a clear indication of how many footfalls are expected at a wild-life sanctuary on an annual basis, however how to design the memorable tourism experience is left to the creativity of the destination manager.

Time Bound:

The objectives should indicate the movement towards attainment of a desirable condition in the future. The time frame to achieve this should be provided. Time bound objectives can provide a direction to the destination manager to develop an action plan that also takes accountability into consideration.

Inference: Example 1 and 3 have specified the duration within which the objective is to be met, while the implementation, creativity to design, develop the plan of action is all the onus of the destination manager.

Implementation of the plan

This stage involves the actor of the plan, ideally the onus is on the destination manager. Implementation of the plan means that all the necessary inputs are already derived from Tier 1 to Tier 9. The road map to the goals are clearly defined and a proper monitoring is also set up to check on the implementation of the plan as it progresses.

Implementation is a necessary stage that helps assess the success or failure of the plan. According to the purpose of the plan these are some of the actions required. For a destination manager whose purpose if organisational development implementation will be associated with creativity in order to achieve the specified objectives and goals. At a community level, the involvement of the local community in providing quality products and service to the visitors and tourist within the guidelines and framework of the policy document. Whereas a well-developed tourism product will ensure that the product is staged well for the visitors and tourist and exported to other countries and regions for consumption. The tourism product marketing implementation will involve activation of the 5P's of marketing and create a destination image in the minds of travelers who are in the process of deciding which destination is best suited for them.

It is not just enough to implement the plan, periodically the plan has to be revisited and the progress has to be monitored and reported to the funding bodies as well as to the top tier levels so that the funding may continue as per the success of the plan. If there are deviations to the implementation due to changes in circumstances such factors have to be accounted for and revisions to the existing plan have to be reported.

Questions:

1. Planning to fail or fail to plan. Discuss on this phrase.

2. Why are implementation and evaluation important phases in the planning process?

Managerial Implications:

 Some additional factors to be considered are the triple bottom line and the return of investment for these aspects. When the socio-cultural development of the local communities is enhanced through implementation of the plan the returns may not just be a short term economic gain, but a sustained and long term means of livelihood and income, as the plans are also set for a longer duration. A successful plan can be further replicated and scaled up in other destinations that require such assistance. When all efforts are made to conserve the ecological balance, the overall health of the destination is also maintained due to the inter-dependence of both human society and the environment. So return on investment may not be monitory gains but also improvement in the overall health of the destination in the long run.

References:

1. Abernathy, W. J., & Clark, K. B. (1985). Innovation: Mapping the winds of creative destruction. Research Policy, 14, 3–22.

2. Adam, M. (1994) Entrepreneurial characteristics of independent hotels and restaurants, in: Proceedings of 3rd CHME Annual Hospitality Research Conference,Edinburgh: Napier University.

3. Andereck, Kathleen L. "Tourists' Perceptions of Environmentally Responsible Innovations at Tourism Businesses." Journal of Sustainable Tourism 17, no. 4 (June 26, 2009): 489–99. https://doi.org/10.1080/09669580802495790.

4. Buhalis, D. (1994) ITT as a strategic tool for DMTEs in the contemporary business environment, in: A. Seaton (Ed.) Tourism: State of the Art, Chichester: Wiley.

5. Buhalis, D. and Main, H. (1996) Information technology in small/independent Welsh and Aegean hotels, in: Proceedings of Hospitality Information Technology Association, Third World-wide Annual Conference (Edinburgh: Napier University).

6. Brittanica (2020). Thomas Cook British Businessman retrieved from

   https://www.britannica.com/biography/Thomas-Cook

7. Chaney, Edward. (2000). The evolution of the grand tour: Anglo-Italian cultural relations since the Renaissance. Portland OR: Routledge.

8. Charmaz, K. (2011). Grounded theory methods in social justice research. In N. K. Denzin & Y. S.

9. Cox and Kings (2020). About Us. Retrieved from

   https://www.coxandkings.com/about-us/index.shtml

10. Expedia, Inc. (2013). Expedia: Annual report 2013. Retrieved from

    http://files.shareholder.com/downloads/EXPE/3546131959x0x750253/

48AF365A-F894-4E9C-8F4A-

8AB11FEE8D2A/EXPE_2013_Annual_Report.PDF

11. Lincoln (Eds.), The 4th Sage handbook of qualitative research, pp. 359–380.

12. David Weaver (2006) Sustainable Tourism: Theory and Practice, Elsevier Butterworth-Heinemann, Oxford

13. Dias, C (2020) Do Grafted Tourism Policies Tick? Conference paper at the Fifth International Scientific Conference Knowledge Based Sustainable Development, ERAZ 2019, Budapest, Hungary

14. Dodds, Rachel. "Introduction: Innovations in Sustainable Tourism." Téoros. Revue de Recherche En Tourisme 31, no. 31, 3 (HS) (August 3, 2012). http://journals.openedition.org/teoros/1995.

15. Eagles, Paul F.J., McCool, Stephen F. and Haynes, Christopher D.A. (2002).

16. Evans, G. (1999) Networking for growth and digital business: local urban tourism SNITEs and ICT, in: D. Buhalis and W. Schertler (Eds) Information and Communications Technologies in Tourism Vienna: Springer-Verlag.

17. Getz, D. (1983). Capacity to absorb tourism: Concepts and implications for strategic planning. *Annals of Tourism Research*, 10:2, pp.239-263

18. Gibson, L., Lynch, P. A., & Morrison, A. (2005). *The local destination tourism network: Development issues. Tourism and Hospitality Planning & Development, 2(2), 87–99.* doi:10.1080/14790530500171708

19. Goeldner, C. R., and Ritchie, B. J. R. (2008). Tourism policy: Structure, content, and process. In Tourism: Principles, Practices, Philosophies (11th ed., pp. 412–416). Wiley.

20. Gustav Wiedsvej 10, 8000 Aarhus C, Denmark, Received 26 October 2001; accepted 24 December 2001, Toursim Management, Pergamon Tourism Management 23 (2002) 465–474

21. Hankinson, A. (1989) Small hotels in Britain: investment and survival, The Cornell HRA Quarterly, 30(3), pp. 80–2.

22. Hjalager, A-M (2002).Repairing Innovation Defectiveness in Tourism. *Tourism Management* 23, no. 5 , pp.465-74. https://doi.org/10.1016/s0261-5177(02)00013-4.

23. Houghton, J. and Tremblay, P. (1995) The structure of hospitality: a cultural explanation of industrial diversity, *International Journal of Hospitality Management*, 13(4), pp. 327–46.

24. Huang, Y. and Stewart, W. D. (1996). Rural tourism development: shifting basis of community solidarity, *Journal of Tourism Research*, 34(4), pp. 26–9.

25. Kennell, J., 2016. Carrying capacity. *Encyclopedia of Tourism* (pp. 133-135). Springer International Publishing. Learning Destination Project, Representatives of Scottish-Scandinavian University Tourism Departments.

26. Litteljohn, D., Foley,M. and Lennon, J. (1996) The potential of accommodation consortia in theHighlands and Islands of Scotland, in: Proceedings of IAHMS Spring Symposium, pp. 55–66 Leeds: Leeds Metropolitan University.

27. Lowe, A. (1988) Small hotel survival: an inductive approach, *International Journal of Hospitality Management*,7(3), pp. 197–223.

28. Lynch, P. A. (2000) Networking in the homestay sector, *The Services Industries Journal*, 20(3), pp. 95–116.

29. Lynch, P., Halcro, K., Johns, N. and Buick, I. (2000) Developing small business networks to build profitable tourist destinations. Paper presented at Destination Development Conference, Ö stersund, Mid-Sweden University, 13–14 September.

30. Markides, C (2006). Disruptive Innovation: In Need of Better Theory. *Journal of Product Innovation Management* 23, no. 1 pp.19-25. https://doi.org/10.1111/j.1540-5885.2005.00177.x.

31. Matteucci, X., and Gnoth, J. (2017). Elaborating on grounded theory in tourism research. *Annals of Tourism Research*, 65(), 49–59. doi:10.1016/j.annals.2017.05.003

32. Morrison, A. (1994) Small tourism business: product distribution system, in: Proceedings of 3rd CHME Annual Hospitality Research Conference (Edinburgh: Napier University).

33. Morrison, A. (1996) Marketing strategic alliances: the small hotel firm, in: Proceedings of IAHMS Spring Symposium, pp. 19–28 (Leeds: Leeds Metropolitan University).

34. Muangasame, K., and McKercher,B. (2014) The challenge of implementing sustainable tourism policy: a 360-degree assessment of

Thailand's "7 Greens sustainable tourism policy", *Journal of Sustainable Tourism*, DOI: 10.1080/09669582.2014.978789

35. Munar, A. and Jamal, T. (2016), "What are Paradigms for?", *Tourism Research Paradigms: Critical and Emergent Knowledges (Tourism Social Science Series, Vol. 22)*, Emerald Group Publishing Limited, pp. 1-16. https://doi.org/10.1108/S1571-504320150000022020

36. Murphy, P. (1985). Tourism: A Community Approach (RLE Tourism) (1st ed.). Routledge. https://doi.org/10.4324/9780203068533

37. NITI Aayog (2019) *SDX India,* retrieved on 10th June 2019, retrieved from https://niti.gov.in/content/sdg-india-index-baseline-report-2018

38. Parekh,A. (2018) *Indian Polity and Constitution,* (1st ed.). Himalaya Publishing House, Mumbai

39. Pavlić, I., & Portolan, A. (2016). *Irritation index. Encyclopedia of Tourism, 495–495.* doi:10.1007/978-3-319-01384-8_564

40. Plog, S. (2001). Why destination areas rise and fall in popularity: an update of a Cornell Quarterly classic. *The Cornell Hotel and Restaurant Administration Quarterly, 42(3), 13–24.* doi:10.1016/s0010-8804(01)81020-x

41. R.W. Butler, "The concept of tourism area cycle of evolution: implications for management of resources", Canadian Geographer 24, 1980, pp.5-12.

42. Scottish-Scandinavian Discussion Group (2001) Unpublished notes of meetings of Networks Sub-Group of Sears,

43. Greg J., and Vishwanath V. Baba. (2011). Toward a Multistage, Multilevel Theory of Innovation. *Canadian Journal of Administrative Sciences* / Revue Canadienne Des Sciences De l'Administration 28, no. 4 , 357-72. https://doi.org/10.1002/cjas.198.

44. Sheller, M., & Urry, J. (2006). The New Mobilities Paradigm. Environment and Planning A, 38(2), 207–226

45. Sørensen, F. (2007). The geographies of social networks and innovation in tourism. *Tourism Geographies*, 9(1), 22–48.

46. Spanoudis, C. (1982). Trends in tourism planning and development. Tourism Management, 3, 314-318.

47. Sustainable Tourism for Development Guidebook (2013) First edition: 2013

48. Sustainable Tourism in Protected Areas: Guidelines for Planning and Management. IUCN Gland, Switzerland and Cambridge, UK. Pp.183

49. Tribe, J., Dann, G., & Jamal, T. (2015). *Paradigms in tourism research: a trialogue. Tourism Recreation Research, 40(1), 28–47.* doi:10.1080/02508281.2015.1008856

50. Turner, D. (2016). What actually is grounded theory? A brief introduction. https://www.Quirkos.Com/Blog/Post/Qualitative-Grounded-Theory-Overview/.

51. UNWTO (1981), *Saturation of Tourist Destinations: Report of the Secretary General*, World Tourism Organisation, Madrid.

52. Urry, J. (2000). Sociology beyond societies: Mobilities for the twenty-first century. London: Routledge

53. Urry, J. (2002). The Tourist Gaze. London: Sage.

54. World Tourism Organization (2020), Framework Convention on Tourism Ethics, UNWTO, Madrid, DOI: https://doi.org/10.18111/9789284421671.

ABOUT THE AUTHOR

Ph.D. from Bharathiar University, with first Class MBA in Human Resource Management from Pondicherry University, UGC NET qualified in HRM, Personal Management, Industrial Relations and Labour Laws. Holds an international diploma as an instructor for both IATA Foundation in Travel and Tourism (DTTF) and IATA Travel and Tourism Consultant (DTTC) courses from ITDI Montreal, Canada. Recipient of 'Kamal Sharma Academic Excellence Award' by Lexicon Group of Institutions in 2021 on 5th September 2021. Recipient of 'Academic Excellence' and 'Research Excellence' awards by InSC in 2020. Recipient of four international best paper awards by RDA, Jaipur, Rajasthan. Recipient of Prestigious President Guide award. Has nine years of teaching experience at Post Graduate Level as a tenured faculty for Masters of Tourism and Travel Management (MTTM), M.A. (Tourism and Heritage Management) at S.S. Dempo College of Commerce and Economics, Goa, and as a visiting faculty for PGDBA-Event Management and M.Com. Served as a visiting faculty for National Institute of Water Sports, IGNTU for a four credit paper in Tourism. Life-time member of Research Development Authority, Jaipur, Rajasthan. Member of Board of Studies for hospitality and tourism, at Goa University. Presented in eleven international conferences, two national conference and published in eleven peer reviewed journals, edited a national level book, and contributed chapter in an international book and national-level book on tourism. Also has a corporate experience of twelve years and worked with reputed international airlines such as Czech Airline and Qatar Airways, and MNC's such as Thomas Cook, Siemens, and TRX. Manager instructional designer at TATA Interactive systems, Mumbai. Provided consultancy services to set up IATA authorised training center at S.S Dempo College of Commerce and Economics. Member of the Scientific (Program) Committee of the ERAZ conferences organised in Europe. Writer on opinion section and letters to the editor in a leading newspaper in Goa. Actively involved in solid waste management and capacity building as a president of a NGO, Eco-Kshatriya Foundation. Subjects of interest are research on women studies, talent development, tourism accessibility, public private partnership in tourism, innovative teaching methods, and trends in the tourism industry.

www.ingramcontent.com/pod-product-compliance
Lightning Source LLC
Chambersburg PA
CBHW071039250726

48653CB00005B/1901